CAMBRIDGE LIBRARY COLLECTION

Books of enduring scholarly value

British and Irish History, Seventeenth and Eighteenth Centuries

The books in this series focus on the British Isles in the early modern period, as interpreted by eighteenth- and nineteenth-century historians, and show the shift to 'scientific' historiography. Several of them are devoted exclusively to the history of Ireland, while others cover topics including economic history, foreign and colonial policy, agriculture and the industrial revolution. There are also works in political thought and social theory, which address subjects such as human rights, the role of women, and criminal justice.

Memoranda, or, Chronicles of the Foundling Hospital

Captain Coram's Foundling Hospital was established in 1739 for 'the maintenance and education of exposed and deserted young children'. Hogarth was a governor of the hospital – he donated several pictures, including his portrait of Coram – as was Handel, whose famous performances of his oratorio *Messiah* were given there from 1750 to raise funds. John Brownlow (1800–73), himself a foundling, was secretary of the hospital from 1849 until his retirement. He introduced improvements to the children's education and was a staunch defender of the hospital, countering the criticism often levelled in the nineteenth century that taking in illegitimate children simply encouraged neglect. Brownlow's *Memoranda*, first published in 1847, presents a valuable account of the hospital, its early supporters, and Coram, as well as descriptions of the paintings (Kneller's portrait of Handel among them) which formed the first public art gallery in London. The book also includes contemporary engravings and facsimiles of many original documents.

Cambridge University Press has long been a pioneer in the reissuing of out-of-print titles from its own backlist, producing digital reprints of books that are still sought after by scholars and students but could not be reprinted economically using traditional technology. The Cambridge Library Collection extends this activity to a wider range of books which are still of importance to researchers and professionals, either for the source material they contain, or as landmarks in the history of their academic discipline.

Drawing from the world-renowned collections in the Cambridge University Library and other partner libraries, and guided by the advice of experts in each subject area, Cambridge University Press is using state-of-the-art scanning machines in its own Printing House to capture the content of each book selected for inclusion. The files are processed to give a consistently clear, crisp image, and the books finished to the high quality standard for which the Press is recognised around the world. The latest print-on-demand technology ensures that the books will remain available indefinitely, and that orders for single or multiple copies can quickly be supplied.

The Cambridge Library Collection brings back to life books of enduring scholarly value (including out-of-copyright works originally issued by other publishers) across a wide range of disciplines in the humanities and social sciences and in science and technology.

Memoranda, or, Chronicles of the Foundling Hospital

Including Memoirs of Captain Coram

John Brownlow

Cambridge
University Press

CAMBRIDGE UNIVERSITY PRESS

Cambridge, New York, Melbourne, Madrid, Cape Town,
Singapore, São Paolo, Delhi, Mexico City

Published in the United States of America by Cambridge University Press, New York

www.cambridge.org
Information on this title: www.cambridge.org/9781108054836

This edition first published 1847
This digitally printed version 2013

ISBN 978-1-108-05483-6 Paperback

Thomas Coram

Painted by Wm. Hogarth Engraved by J. W. Cook.

MEMORANDA;

OR,

CHRONICLES

OF

THE FOUNDLING HOSPITAL,

INCLUDING

MEMOIRS OF CAPTAIN CORAM,

&c. &c.

By JOHN BROWNLOW.

LONDON:

SAMPSON LOW, LAMBS CONDUIT STREET.

1847.

CONTENTS.

Directions to the Binder.

MEMORANDA,

FOUNDLING HOSPITAL.

Sir Robert Strange in his "Enquiry into the rise and Establishment of the Royal Academy of Arts," makes the following remark.—

"The donations in painting, which several artists presented to the *Foundling Hospital*, were among the first objects of this nature, which had engaged the attention of the public. The artists, observing the effects that these paintings produced, came, in the year 1760, to a resolution to try the fate of an exhibition of their works. This effort had its desired effect: the public were entertained, and the artists were excited to emulation."—

And again in his "Conduct of the Royal Academicians," he says,

"Accident has often been observed to produce, what the utmost efforts of industry have failed to accomplish; and something of that kind seems to have happened here. As liberty has ever been considered the friend and parent of the fine arts, it is natural for their professors to revere the memory of all those who were the champions and assertors of that invaluable blessing, particularly those of our own country: on this principle it was, that the artists we are now speaking of, had an annual meeting at the *Foundling Hospital,* to commemorate the landing of King William. To this charity, several of their body had made donations in Painting, Sculpture, &c. which being accessible to the public, made those artists more generally known than others; and this circumstance it was, that first suggested an exhibition; which was no sooner proposed than approved; the Committee consequently, who were the proposers, received directions to issue proper notices of the intention; the performances of many ingenious men, hitherto unknown, were received, and on the 21st day of April, 1760, an exhibition was opened in the great room, belonging to the Society of Arts, Manufactures and Commerce, in the Strand; on which it will be sufficient to observe, that the success was equal to the most sanguine expectations; the public were pleased, and the artists applauded; those already known received additional reputation, and such as were not, became the immediate acquaintance of the public."

Edwards also in his anecdotes, of Painters, speaking of the unsuccessful attempts made to form an Academy, says,

"Although these endeavours of the artists had not succeeded, they were far from being so discouraged as not to continue their meetings, as well as their studies; and the next effort they made, towards acquiring the attention of the public, was connected with the *Foundling Hospital.*

"This Institution, so humane in its primitive intention, whatever may be thought of its effects, was incorporated by Charter, dated 1739. A few years after that period, the present building was erected; but as the income of the Charity could, with no propriety, be expended upon decorations, many of the principal artists of that day voluntarily exerted their talents for the purpose of ornamenting several of the apartments of the Hospital, which otherwise must have remained without decoration. The pictures thus produced, and generously given, were permitted to be seen by any visitor, upon proper application. The spectacle was so new, that it made a considerable impression upon the public, and the favorable reception these works experienced, impressed the artists with an idea of forming a public exhibition."

Of the period referred to, Smollett, in his History of the Reign of George II. remarks,

"The British soil, which had hitherto been barren in the article of painting, now produced some artists of extraordinary merit. Hogarth excelled all the world in exhibiting the scenes of ordinary life; in humour, character, and expression. Hayman became eminent for historical designs and conversation pieces. Reynolds and Ramsay distinguished themselves by their superior merits in portraits; a branch that was successfully cultivated by many other English painters. Wootton was famous for representing live animals in general; Seymour for racehorses; Lambert and the Smiths for landscapes; and Scott for sea peices. Several spirited attempts were made on historical subjects, but little progress was made in the sublime parts of painting. Essays of this kind were discouraged by a false taste, founded upon a reprobation of British genius. The art of engraving was brought to perfection by Strange, and laudably practised by Grignon, Baron, Ravenet, and several other masters: great improvements were made in mezzotinto, miniature and enamel. Many fair monuments of sculpture or statuary were raised by Rysbrach, Roubilliac and Wilton.

Architecture, which had been cherished by the elegant taste of Burlington, soon became a favourite study, and many magnificent edifices were reared in different parts of the kingdom."

Another writer has said, "that it is within the Walls of the *Foundling* the curious may contemplate the state of British art previously to the epoch when George the III. first countenanced the historical talent of West."

With such evidence as is afforded by these statements of the peculiar interest attached to the progress of the arts in the Reign of George the II., and of their partial association with the institution of the *Foundling Hospital*, it seems right that if any thing remains to be told on such a subject (however small), it should not be withheld.

It is therefore with a view of collecting together a few scattered materials not hitherto published, and of recording in a concentrated form, events long since past, of which the Hospital has been the scene, and the History of Men who have laboured in its vineyard, that this Book is compiled.

The establishment of a Foundling Hospital in England, now upwards of 100 years ago, took a strong hold on the national sympathy: it immediately became what is termed a "popular" Institution. The then ill-defined and wretched administration of the Poor Laws, left the deserted child without other protection than the casual humanity of the passenger—lives were lost to the commonwealth by this absence of public feeling, wisdom, and forethought. Men, therefore, of kindly disposition, joined in this enlarged work of Charity, not because they were insensible of its partially mischievous tendency, but because they conceived that the contemplated salvation of numerous lives to the public was paramount to any evil which might arise from it.

Amongst those who co-operated in forwarding this work of extended humanity, was the celebrated painter, William Hogarth, and by the Charter for incorporating the Hospital, he appears as one of its constituent members, under the denomination of "a Governor and Guardian," along with a host of other "trusty and well-beloved subjects" of his Majesty, George the II.

Nor did Hogarth hold this appointment to be merely nominal, for we find him subscribing his money, and attending the Courts or General Meetings at the Hospital, as one of its active members, and joining heartily in carrying out the designs of his friend, the venerable Captain Coram, through whose zeal and humanity the Hospital was founded.

The Charter of the Hospital authorized the Governors to appoint persons to ask for alms on behalf of the Charity and to receive Subscriptions; and the first artistical work of Hogarth in aid of this object, was to prepare a "head piece" to a Power of Attorney drawn up for the purpose: a copy of which head piece is annexed, taken from the original plate in the possession of the Hospital, and now for the first time published by the kind permission of the present Governors.

The principal figure is that of Captain Coram himself, with the Charter under his arm. Before him the beadle carries an Infant, whose mother having dropped a dagger with which she might have been momentarily tempted to destroy her child, kneels at his feet, while he, with that benevolence with which his countenance is so eminently marked, bids her be comforted, for her babe will be nursed and protected. On the dexter side of the print is a new born Infant left close to a stream of water which runs under the arch of a bridge. Near a gate on a little eminence in the pathway above, a woman leaves another child to the casual care of the next person who passes by. In the distance is a village with a Church. In the other corner are three boys coming out of the door, with the King's Arms over it, with emblems of their future employments—one of them poises a plummet —a second holds a trowel, and a third, whose mother is fondly pressing him to her bosom, has in his hand

W. Hogarth inv. F. Morellon La Cave Sculp London.

a card for combing wool. The next group, headed by a lad elevating a mathematical instrument, are in sailors jackets and trousers. Those on their right hand, one of whom has a rake, are in the uniform of the school. The attributes of the three little girls in the foreground—a spinning-wheel, a sampler and broom, indicate female industry and ingenuity.

It should be remarked that the designs of the Hospital, foreshadowed by this interesting engraving, did not come into actual operation 'till two years afterwards.

In May, 1740, that is, seven months after the granting of the Charter, at the Annual Court, "Mr. Folkes * acquainted the Governors, that Mr. Hogarth

---

* Martin Folkes, Esq. (a Vice-President of the Hospital).

This elegant scholar was a Mathematician and Antiquary of much celebrity in the philosophical annals of literature. In 1713, at the early age of twenty-four, he was elected a Fellow of the Royal Society, and in 1741 was elected President. Mr. Folkes was also an early Member of the Society of Antiquaries, having been elected in 1719–20, and his communications to both Societies were numerous and valuable. His knowledge in ancient and modern coins was very extensive; and the most important work he produced, was "The History of the English Gold and Silver Coin, from the Conquest to his own time." Algernon, the famous Duke of Somerset, who had been many years President of the Society of Antiquaries, dying February 9, 1749–50, Mr. Folkes, who was then one of the Vice-Presidents, was immediately chosen to succeed his Grace; and was continued President by the Charter of Incorporation of that Society, November 2, 1751. But he was soon disabled from presiding in person, either in that or the Royal Society, being seized on the 26th September, the same year, with a palsy, which deprived him of the use of his left side. On the 30th November, 1753, he resigned the Presidentship of the Royal Society, but continued President of the Society of Antiquaries till his death. After having languished nearly three years, a second attack of his disorder, on the 25th June, 1754, put an end to his life on the 28th of that month. His portrait, painted by Hogarth, is in the Council room of the Royal Society.

had presented to them a whole length picture of Mr. Coram, for this Corporation to keep in memory of the said Mr. Coram's having solicited, and obtained His Majesty's Royal Charter for this Charity." Writing of himself some years afterwards, Hogarth says " The portrait which I painted with most pleasure, and in which I particularly wished to excel, was that of Captain Coram for the *Foundling Hospital*; and" (he adds in allusion to his detractors as a portrait painter) "if I am so wretched an artist as my enemies assert, it is somewhat strange that this, which was one of the first I painted the size of life, should stand the test of twenty years competition, and be generally thought the best portrait in the place, notwithstanding the first painters in the kingdom exerted all their talents to vie with it."*

Hogarth is said to have displayed no little vanity regarding his pretensions as a portrait painter. In proof of this, it is related of him, that being at dinner with Dr. Cheselden, and some other company, he was informed that John Freke, surgeon of St. Bartholomew's Hospital, had asserted in Dick's Coffee House, that Greene was as eminent in composition as Handel. "That fellow, Freke," cried Hogarth, "is always shooting his bolt absurdly one way or another. Handel is a giant in music, Greene only a

---

* The rival portraits here alluded to, are George the Second, Patron of the Foundation, by Shackleton; Lord Dartmouth, one of the Vice-Presidents, by Mr Reynolds, (afterwards *Sir Joshua*); Taylor White, Treasurer of the Hospital, in crayons, by Cotes; Mr. Milner and Mr. Jacobson, by Hudson; Dr. Mead, by Ramsay; Mr. Emmerson, by Highmore; and Francis Fanquier, Esq., by Wilson.

HELP

light Florimel kind of composer." "Aye, but" said the other, "Freke declared you were as good a portrait painter as Vandyck." "There he was in the right," quoth Hogarth, "and so I am, give me but my time and let me choose my subject."

In March, 1741, the Governors resolved to commence upon the good purposes of their Charter, but not being able to obtain a suitable building, they took houses in Hatton Garden, near the Charity School, and opened them as receptacles and nurseries for Infants. In the minutes of that month is the following entry:—

"Mr. Taylor White acquainted the Committee that Mr. Hogarth had painted a Shield which was put up over the door of this Hospital, and presented the same to this Hospital."

This shield, or sign, has not been preserved, nor is there any record of its design, but it is not improbable that it was an emblematical sketch similar in character, if not actually the same, as the Arms of the Hospital presented to the Court of Governors, by the Authorities of the Heralds' College, in 1747, and which is said by Nichols, in his Biographical Anecdotes, to have been designed by Hogarth. The technical description of these Arms is as follows, viz.

"Party per fesse, Azure & Vert," a young child lying naked and exposed, extending its right hand proper. In chief a Crescent Argent between two Mullets of six points Or; and for a Crest on a Wreath of the Colours, a Lamb Argent, holding in its mouth a Sprig of Thyme proper, supported on the dexter side by a terminal figure of a Woman full of Nipples proper, with a Mantle Vert, the term Argent being the emblem of Liberty, represented by Britannia holding in her right hand upon a staff proper, a a Cap Argent, and habited in a Vest Azure, girt with belt Or, the under garment Gules." Motto "Help."

The Governors of the Charity having purchased fifty-six acres of land of the Earl of Salisbury, commenced in 1740 erecting the present Building, the western wing of which was finished and inhabited in 1745. It was at this period that Hogarth contemplated the adornment of its walls with works of Art, with which view he solicited and obtained the co-operation of some of his professional brethren. At a Court of Governors, held on the 31st December, 1746, Hogarth, and Rysbrach, the sculptor, being present as Governors of the Hospital,—"The Treasurer acquainted this General Meeting, that the following Gentlemen, Artists, had severally presented, and agreed to present, performances in their different professions, for ornamenting this Hospital, viz. Mr. Francis Hayman, Mr. James Wills, Mr. Joseph Highmore, Mr. Thomas Hudson, Mr. Allan Ramsay, Mr. George Lambert, Mr. Samuel Scott, Mr. Peter Monamy, Mr. Richard Wilson, Mr. Samuel Whale, Mr. Edward Hately, Mr. Thomas Carter, Mr. George Moser, Mr. Robert Taylor, and Mr. John Pyne, Whereupon this General Meeting elected, by ballot, the said Mr. Francis Hayman, Mr. James Wills, Mr. Joseph Highmore, Mr. Thomas Hudson, Mr. Allan Ramsay, Mr. George Lambert, Mr. Samuel

Scott, Mr. Peter Monamy, Mr. Richard Wilson, Mr. Samuel Whale, Mr. Edward Hately, Mr. Thomas Carter, Mr. George Moser, Mr. Robert Taylor, and Mr. John Pyne, Governors and Guardians of this Hospital.

" *Resolved,—*

"That the said Artists, and Mr. Hogarth, Mr. Zinke, Mr. Rysbrach, and Mr. Jacobson, or any three or more of them, be a Committee to meet annually on the 5th of November, to consider of what further ornaments may be added to this Hospital, without any expense to the Charity."

Whether these artists were previously associated as a Society elsewhere for the promotion of the Arts, or for conviviality, does not appear, or whether they began to form themselves from this time and out of this occasion, cannot be determined, but it seems probable that they were part of a Society alluded to by Edwards, who says, "of the Dilettante Society, the author is not sufficiently informed to give a perfect account, and therefore can only relate the following circumstances. Its original institution was prior to either of those already mentioned. It commenced upon political principles, and, as far as it was then known to the public, was not approved, being considered as rather a disaffected assembly. But they soon changed the object of their meetings and turned their attention to the encouragement of the Arts, and made some attempts to assist in the establishment of a public academy."

Assuming that the artists who thus proposed to

hold an annual meeting at the Hospital, belonged to the Dilettante Society, it may be said that whatever their previous objects or bias might have been, their present purpose, notwithstanding the ominousness of the day fixed on for their meetings (viz. the 5th of November), originated in as harmless a conspiracy as could be devised, that of plotting for the advancement of the Arts, and of a public Charity.

It seems that these meetings, which commenced with the modest suggestion "that any three or more of them be a Committee," grew so mightily, that that which was intended to be a mere matter of business, ended (as most associations of Englishmen do) in an occasion of conviviality, and that on the 5th of November of each succeeding year, and for many years, the artists of the day, and the patronizers of the Arts, dined at the Hospital.*

In the mean time, the donations in painting, &c., the result of these meetings, increased, and "being exhibited to the public, drew a daily crowd of spectators in their splendid equipages; and a visit to the Foundling became the most fashionable morning lounge of the Reign of George II. The *eclât* thus excited in favor of the Arts, suggested the annual exhibition of the united artists, which Institution was the precursor of the Royal Academy."†

Hogarth was not only the principal contributor,

* These Festivals were altogether distinct from similar meetings of the Governors themselves, which were held on the second Wednesday in May, in each year.

† Vide *Catalogue Raisonne* of West's pictures.

Standidge & Co. Lithe. London

South View of the Foundling Hospital, 1749.

but the leader of his brethren in all that related to ornamenting the Hospital, and therefore it is as much due to his benevolence and generosity, as to his distinguished talents, that his further connexion with the Institution should receive special notice in this compilation.

At a Court of Governors on the 9th of May, 1750 (Hogarth being present),

"The Treasurer acquainted the General Court, that Mr. Hogarth had presented the Hospital with the remainder of the tickets Mr. Hogarth had left, for the chance of the picture he had painted, of *The March to Finchley,* in the time of the late Rebellion; and that the fortunate number for the said picture being among those tickets, the Hospital had received the said picture.

"*Resolved,—*

"That the thanks of this General Court be given to Mr. Hogarth, for the said benefaction; which the Vice-President accordingly did."

In the "General Advertiser" of the 1st of May, 1750, the same circumstance is thus related.—

"Yesterday Mr. Hogarth's subscription was closed, 1843 chances being subscribed for, Mr. Hogarth gave the remaining 167 chances to the Foundling Hospital, and the same night delivered the picture to the Governors."

Ireland, in his Illustrations of Hogarth, remarks as follows on this subject.—

"By the fortunate number being among those presented to a Charity, which he so much wished to serve, the artist was highly gratified. In a private house, it would have been in a degree secluded from the public, and by the lapse of time, have been transferred to those who could not appreciate its merit, and from either negligence or ignorance, might have been destroyed by damp walls, or effaced from the canvass by picture cleaners. Here, it was likely to remain a permanent and honourable testimony of his talents and liberality. Notwithstanding all this, Hogarth soon after waited upon the Treasurer of the Hospital, and acquainted him that if the Trustees thought proper, they were at liberty to dispose of the picture by auction. His motive for giving this permission it is not easy to assign, they might have their origin in his desire to enrich a foundation, which had his warmest wishes, or a natural, though ill-judged ambition to have his greatest work in the possession of some one who had a collection of the old masters, with whom he in no degree dreaded a competition. Whether his mind was actuated by these, or other causes, is not important; certain it is, that his opinion changed, he requested the trustees would not dispose of it, and never afterwards consented to the measure he himself had originally proposed. The late Duke of Ancaster's father wished to become a purchaser, and once offered the trustees three hundred pounds for it. I have been told, that a much larger sum was since proffered by another gentleman."

It is related in the Gentleman's Magazine, on the authority of an anonymous writer, "that a *Lady* was the possessor of the fortunate number, and intended to present it to the Foundling Hospital. But that some person having suggested what a door would be open to scandal, were any of her sex to make such a present, it was given to Hogarth, on the express condition that it should be presented in his own name."

The next work which Hogarth presented, was "Moses before Pharaoh's Daughter." This was painted expressly for the Hospital, and appears to have originated in a conjoint agreement, between Hayman, Highmore, Wills, and himself, that they should each fill up one of the compartments of the Court Room with pictures, uniform in size, and of suitable subjects taken from Scripture.

The Hospital had thus obtained from Hogarth, a picture in each of the styles of painting which he had attempted, and it may be said, without liability of contradiction, that the best specimens of those styles are within its walls.

It is a somewhat singular circumstance, that as Hogarth throughout his life uniformly opposed the establishment of a Public Academy of Arts, he should, by the very course he pursued in encouraging and concentrating at the Foundling Hospital an exhibition of the talents of British artists, have himself promoted a consummation of the object which he had all along deprecated. "In consequence," says Nichols, "of the public attention bestowed upon the paintings presented to the Foundling Hospital by Hogarth, the academy in St.

Martin's Lane, began to form themselves into a more important body, and to teach the arts under regular professors. But, extraordinary as it may appear, this scheme was so far from being welcomed by Hogarth, as indicative of a brighter era in the Fine Arts, that he absolutely discouraged it, as tending to allure many young men into a profession in which they would not be able to support themselves, and at the same time to degrade what ought to be a liberal profession, into a merely mechanical one."

The annual meetings of the artists at the Hospital were held without interruption for a series of years, and they appear to have increased in importance as time advanced. The purpose with which they commenced had been pursued with charitable ardour, and it is evident that incited by the result (a result unanticipated at the outset), the artists of London were looking forward to other and more important objects. It is true that these meetings were uninfluenced in their origin, except by a simple (tho' noble) motive—the motive of benevolence, but as is often the case in small beginnings, a great *end* was accomplished. Hitherto, the artists of London had existed, as a Society, in *sections* only. At these aggregate meetings they were concentrated as one body, and all that mind had then brought to bear on Art, was diffused in social and edifying converse. Out of this arose the Academy which many of the artists had long cherished the hope of seeing realized. Of those who thus met at the Foundling

Hospital, it may be satisfactory to give one example. The paper from which the names are taken is headed, "5th November, 1757, Dilettante, Virtuosi, Feast."*

It will be seen that the names are not placed in the order of merit, but as they appear accidentally in the original document. There were no less

---

* The Dilettante Society appears by the following account from "Smith's Antiquarian Rambles," to have been remodelled after this period.

"The next object of notoriety is the Thatched House Tavern, so called in 1711. It will long be remembered as the place of meeting of some of the first clubs for rank and talent in England.

"The pictures which adorn the room in which the members of the Dilettante Society hold their meetings, are portraits of many of the members of that Society.

"Over the chimney of a back room, on the first floor, hangs a portrait of Sir Joshua Reynolds, with spectacles on, similar to the one in the Royal collection. This picture was presented by Sir Joshua, as the founder of the Club, which commenced in 1764, at the Turk's Head Tavern, in Gerrard Street, Soho, though the annals are not earlier than April 7th, 1775. The Club, which originally consisted of thirty members, on the 7th May 1780 was augmented to thirty-five, and not to exceed forty.

"On the death of the landlord of the 'Turk's Head,' the club moved, in 1783, to the sign of the 'Prince,' in Sackville Street, from thence to Baxter's, in Dover Street, and then on the 17th January, 1792, to Parsloe's, in St. James's Street, and from thence, on the 26th of February, 1799, to the 'Thatched House,' where it now remains."

The same author also says—"Another Society of Artists met under the auspices of Mr. Moser, in Peter's Court, St. Martin's Lane, from the year 1739 to 1767. After continued squabbles, which had lasted many years, the principal artists, including Benjamin West, Richard Wilson, Edward Penny, Joseph Wilton, Sir William Chambers, G. M. Moser, Paul Sandby, and J. M. Newton, met together at the 'Turk's Head,' where many others having joined them, they agreed to petition the King (George the III.) to become Patron of a Royal Academy of Arts. His Majesty consented, and the new Society took a Room in Pall Mall, opposite to Market Lane, where they remained until the King, in the year 1771, granted them Apartments in Old Somerset House."

than 154 persons, more or less distinguished, who attended on this occasion, viz.—

PAINTERS.

Anrion
Astley
Brooking
Baker
Casali, Chevalier
Cotes, Sen.
Cotes, Jun.
Catton
Cipriani
Chamberlain
Downes
Dawes
Dalton
Evans
Euard
Hayman
Hudson
Hone, Sen.
Hone, Jun.
Haytley
Hogarth
Hamilton
Highmore
Kirby
Keeble
Lambert
Liotard
Luders
Moser (and Chaser)
Meyer
Mathyas
Newton
Pine
Reynolds, Sir Joshua
Richards
Reibenstein
Ramsay
Shackleton
Seere
Scott
Spencer
Stuart
Toms
Wale
Wills, Rev. Mr.
Wilson, Richard
Wilson, B.
Zincke
Zuccarelli.

SCULPTORS.

Collins
Cheere
Carter
Hayward
Read
Roubilliac
Rysbrack
Spang
Tyler
Taylor
Way
Wilton, Sen.
Wilton, Jun.

ARCHITECTS.

Chambers, Sir Wm.
Donowell
Gwynn
Jacobsen
Keene
Payne
Revett
Sanderson
Ware.

ENGRAVERS.

Basire
Chambers
Dacier
Grignion
McArdel
Müller
Major
Rooker
Seaton
Sullivan
Strange, Sir Rt.
Walker
Yeo.

Bedwell
[1]Beard
Bowman
Blackwood
Bencraft
[2]Bonneau
Bayntum
[3]Belchier
Barton
Beckford, Alderman
[4]Cadogan, Dr.
[5]Conyers, Dr.
Crouch
[6]Colbeck
Combs
Carry
Devall
Dingley
Darby
Eaton, Sen.
Eaton, Jun.
Ellys
[7]Forrest, Jun.
Fauquire
Fogg
[8]Freke
[9]Francklin, Dr.
[10]Goodchild
Grosvenor
[11]Hanway, Jonas

---

[1] A celebrated Singer. [2] Drawing Master. [3] Surgeon. [4] Author of a Dissertation on Gout, &c. [5] Physician to the Hospital. [6] Counseller. [7] Friend of Hogarth. [8] Surgeon of St. Bartholomew's Hospital. [9] Translator of Sophocles, &c. [10] One of the Founders of the Society of Arts. [11] The celebrated Philanthropist.

Hatsell
Hawley, Dr.
Hankey, Sir Joseph
Hughes
Ives
[1]Lockman
[2]Langford
Mead, Jun.
[3]Morton, Dr.
Ongley
Partington
Phillips
[4]Reynardson
Reydezel, Baron
Radclif
Rowe
[5]Stukeley, Dr.
Stevens
Saunders
[6]Scott
Scarlet
Spencer
Stuart, Captain
[7]Smith
Sherif, Tom
[8]Tomkyns
Trent, Rev. Mr.
[9]Tonson
[10]Tindal
Vere
Vernon
Wilder
[11]White
[12]Whatley
Wynde
Woodward
Webb
Williams
Wegg
[13]Welsh, Justice.

There is a halo surrounding the past, especially when associated with men of talent, which brings many pleasing, though, perhaps, exaggerated feelings. It is this which causes us to regret our limited acquaintance with their habits and conversation, and often could we desire that at every congregation of genius and talent, a Boswell was present to hand down to us their words and their

[1] Translator of Poree's Oration, &c. [2] Auctioneer. [3] Principal Librarian of British Museum. [4] Fellow of the Society of Arts at the time of its Incorporation. [5] Celebrated Antiquary. [6] Organist. [7] First Organist of the Foundling Chapel, and Amanuensis to Handel. [8] Surgeon of the Hospital. [9] Bookseller. [10] Printer. [11] Treasurer of the Hospital. [12] An Active Governor, and afterwards Treasurer. [13] Friend of Hogarth, and Father-in-Law to Nollekins, the Sculptor.

wit, so as to bring them in closer union with us. But this is not the fortuitous lot of every great man (as it was that of Dr. Johnson), and therefore we are left to our imagination to supply the space which is void by the absence of facts. Such is the case with these meetings of the artists at the Foundling Hospital.

In the course of this work a succinct account will be given of several of the most eminent of them, and of their Donations to the Hospital. There are others in the list, whose history is now almost forgotten, and therefore the following gleanings of a few of them may be interesting. Though dazzled by the luminaries in art of these days, we must not forget that their fires have been kindled by the lesser lights of the past.

* JOHN ASTLEY.—Was born at Wem, in Shropshire, and received his early education in the country. His father was of the medical profession. When of age to assume a profession himself, he was sent to London, and placed as a pupil under the care of Hudson. It is not known how long he staid with his master, but when he left him he visited Rome, and was there about the same time with Sir Joshua Reynolds. After his return to England, he resided at a friend's house for some months in London, and from thence went to Dublin, where he practised as a painter for about three years, and in that

---

* These Biographical Notices are extracted, for the most part, from Edwards's "Anecdotes of Painters," long since out of print.

time acquired three thousand pounds by his pencil. His next adventure is narrated in the words of one who was well acquainted with him. "As he was painting his way back to London, in his own post-chaise, with an out-rider, he loitered with a little pardonable vanity in his native neighbourhood, and visiting Nutsford Assembly, with another gentleman, Lady Daniel, a widow then present, was at once so won by his appearance, that she contrived to sit to him for her portrait, and then made him the offer of her hand, a boon which he did not think it prudent to refuse." In the decline of his life, he appeared to be disturbed by reflections upon the dissipated conduct of his early days, and when near his end, was not without apprehension of being reduced to indigence and want. He died at his house, Duckenfield Lodge, Cheshire, 14th November, 1787, and was buried at the church of that village.

John Baker.—A painter of flowers, was chiefly employed in ornamenting coaches, and had been regularly bred a coach-painter. At the foundation of the Royal Academy he was chosen one of the members, but did not long enjoy that honour, for he died in the year 1771.

Charles Catton.—Was born at Norwich, and apprenticed to a coach-painter in London, of the name of Maxfield. With a laudable ambition to improve his talents in art, he became a member of the Academy in St. Martin's Lane, where he acquired a knowledge of the human figure, which, together with his natural taste, ranked him above all others of his profession in London. He was the first Herald-painter who ventured to correct the bad manner of painting the supporters of coats of arms, which had long been the practice of his predecessors, whose representations of animals are considered as heraldic fictions rather than the resemblances of animated nature. At the foundation of the Royal Academy he was appointed one of the members.

JOHN BAPTIST CIPRIANI.—Descended from an ancient family in Florence, where he was born. He received his first instruction from an English artist of the name of Heckford, who had settled in that city, and afterwards went under the tuition of Gabiani, a painter of celebrity at that time in Italy. In August, 1755, he came to England with Wilton and Sir William Chambers, on their return from the Continent, and was patronized in this country by the late Earl of Tilney. At the foundation of the Royal Academy, he was chosen one of the members; he was also employed to make the design for the diploma which is given to the academicians and associates at their admission to the Society. This work he executed with great taste and elegance. For this he received a Silver Cup, upon which was engraved the following inscription,—"This Cup is presented to J. B. Cipriani, R.A. by the President and Council of the Royal Academy of Arts in London, as an acknowledgment for the assistance the Academy has received from his great abilities in his profession."

Mason Chamberlain.—Was employed, in the early part of his life, as a clerk in a merchant's counting-house, but afterwards became the pupil of Hayman. He resided in the vicinity of Spitalfields, where he painted portraits with tolerable success, some of which possess great force and resemblance, as those of Dr. Chandler, and of Mr. Catton the artist, both of which were exhibited. When the Royal Academy was founded he was chosen one of its members. He died in January, 1787.

Cheere.—He succeeded John Van Nost, a statuary, in St. Martin's Lane, in 1739. Cheere served his time to his brother Sir Henry Cheere, the statuary, who executed several monuments in Westminster Abbey.

Richard Dalton.—Was a native of Cumberland, and apprenticed to a coach-painter in Clerkenwell. After quitting his master he went to Rome to pursue the study of painting, where meeting with Lord Charlemont, he was engaged by his Lordship to accompany him to Greece, about the year 1749. On his return to England, he was, by the interest of his noble patron, introduced to the notice of George III. (then Prince of Wales), who, after his accession to the throne, appointed him his librarian. Soon after his appointment, it was determined to form a noble collection of drawings, medals, &c., for which purpose Mr. Dalton was sent to Italy to collect the various articles suited to the intention. The object of his tour being accomplished, he re-visited London, and when the Royal Cabinet was adjusted, his department of librarian was changed to that of keeper of the drawings, and medals. Upon the death of Mr. Knapton, he was by his Majesty appointed surveyor of the pictures in the Palaces. Upon his first appointment at Court he had apartments at St. James's Palace, where he resided till his death, which was in February, 1791. When the Society of Artists was incorporated by Charter, he was appointed the Treasurer, but soon resigned the office, in consequence of the dissensions which took place in that Institution.

Bernard Downes.—Was a portrait painter, who resided in London, and occasionally visited different parts of the country. His name stands in the second exhibition catalogue and is continued till the year 1775, when he ceased to exhibit. He did not long survive.

Philip Dawes.— The natural son of a gentleman in the City, was the pupil of Hogarth, but did not inherit any great portion of his master's spirit, though he endeavoured to tread in his steps. In the year 1760, he was among those artists who became candidates for the premium offered by the Society for the Encouragement of Arts, &c. for the best historical picture; but his exertions were not attended with success, nor did he meet with much employment: on which account his circumstances were rather confined, till the death of his father, who left him a decent competency, which rendered the latter part of his life comfortable. His name stands in the catalogue of the first exhibition, in which was the picture he painted for the premium; the subject, Mortimer taken Prisoner by Edward the Third in Nottingham Castle. In the following year, he also exhibited two pictures at the Room in Spring Gardens; one of them from Johnson's Comedy of "Every Man in his Humour;" the scene, Captain Bobadil cudgelled, from which there is an engraved print. His best pictures bear a resemblance to the manner of his master, and some of them have been dignified with the name of Hogarth; but such misnomers have only betrayed a want of knowledge, or integrity, in those by whom they were thus distinguished. It is not certainly known when he died, but it is supposed before the year 1780.

George Evans.—Practised chiefly as a house-painter, but frequently painted portraits, of which he exhibited a specimen in 1764. He was for some time a member of the private Academy in St. Martin's Lane. He died before the year 1770.

John Gwynn resided in Little Court, Castle Street, Leicester Fields. He was an architect, and built, among other works, the Bridge at Shrewsbury; with which the inhabitants were so much pleased, that a portrait of him was voted to be put up in the Town-hall. He was supported by his steady friend Dr. Johnson, who wrote several powerful letters concerning his talent and integrity; particularly when Gwynn held a long and serious competitorship with Milne for the designing and building Blackfriars Bridge. Gwynn was the professed author of that most ingenious and entertaining work, entitled "London and Westminster Improved." His friend, the Doctor, wrote the preface, and to the credit of this production, the public have availed themselves of his suggestions, and very copiously too, in the late extensive and liberal improvements of New London, for so it must now be considered. Boswell relates a conversation between Gwynn and Dr. Johnson as follows. "Gwynn was a fine lively rattling fellow. Dr. Johnson kept him in subjection, but with a kindly authority. The spirit of the artist, however, rose against what he thought a Gothic attack, and he made a brisk defence. 'What Sir, you will allow no value to beauty in architecture or statuary? Why should we allow it then in writing? Why do you take the trouble to give us so many fine allusions, and bright images, and elegant phrases? You might convey all your instruction without these ornaments.' Johnson smiled with complacency; but said, 'Why, Sir, all these ornaments are useful, because they obtain an easier reception for truth; but a building is not at all more convenient for being decorated with superfluous carved work.' Gwynn at last was lucky enough to make one reply to Dr. Johnson, which he allowed to be excellent. Johnson censured him for taking down a church, which might have stood many years, and building a new one at a different place, for no other reason but that there might be a direct road to a new bridge; and his expression was, 'you are taking a church out of the way, that the people may go in a straight line to the bridge.' 'No, Sir,' said Gwynn, 'I am putting the church *in the way*, that the people may not *go out of the way*.' Johnson (with a hearty loud laugh of approbation) said 'speak no more. Rest your colloquial fame upon this.'"

GAVIN HAMILTON.—A painter of considerable estimation, who practised in history, and sometimes painted portraits. He was of a good family, and was born at Lanark, in North Britain. When young he went to Rome; and was the pupil of Augustine Massuchi. He resided but little in England, though he was certainly settled here about 1752, as there are two prints after pictures which he painted of the Duchess of Hamilton, and her sister, the Countess of Coventry, who were at that time the celebrated beauties of the English Court. He also painted a picture of Mr. Dawkins and Mr. Wood, at their first discovery of the ruins of Palmyra, figures as large as life, from which there is a print engraved by Mr. Hall. After having painted those pictures he returned to Rome, where he resided till the death of his elder brother, when he came to England to take possession of the property which descended to him; but he staid a very short time, as he disliked the country and the climate, and therefore returned to his favourite city, where he continued till his death, which happened in the summer of 1797.

THEODORE JACOBSEN was architect of the Foundling Hospital, and of the Royal Hospital at Gosport. He was fellow of the Royal and Antiquarian Societies, and member of the Arts and Sciences. He died in May, 1772, and was buried in the vault of his family, in Allhallows Church, Thames Street, London.

JOSHUA KIRBY.—Resided in the early part of his life at Ipswich, in Suffolk, where he practised as a coach and house-painter, and where he formed a lasting friendship with Gainsborough. Having a turn for mathematical inquiries, he studied perspective, in which he acquired so much skill, as enabled him to produce and publish a Treatise on that science. This work he dedicated to Hogarth, from whom he obtained a design for the frontispiece. This introduced him to the acquaintance of most of the artists of that time. He also obtained the notice of Mr. Chambers, by whose recommendation he had the honour of instructing George III. (then Prince of Wales) in the science of perspective. He also practised as a landscape painter, and exhibited several pictures, views of different places. When the Chartered Society of Artists was disturbed by the conduct of a party of its members, Mr. Kirby was, by the mal-contents, elected President in the place of Hayman.

WILLIAM KEEBLE.—Was a painter of portraits, and in the year 1754, was a member of the Academy in St. Martin's Lane. There is a mezzotinto print by McArdell, which was executed after a picture painted by Mr. Keeble. It is the whole-length portrait of Sir Crisp Gascoyne, Knight, Lord Mayor of London, in 1753.

JOHN STEPHEN LIOTARD was born at Geneva, in

1702. He came over (says Walpole) in the reign of George II., and stayed two years. He painted admirably well in miniature, and finely in enamel, though he seldom practised it. But he is best known by his works in crayons. His likenesses were as exact as possible, and too like to please those who sat to him: thus he had great business the first year, and very little the second. Devoid of imagination, and one would think of memory also, he could render nothing but what he saw before his eyes. Freckles, marks of the small pox, every thing found its place; not so much from fidelity, as because he could not conceive the absence of anything that appeared to him. Truth prevailed in all his works, grace in very few or none. Nor was there any ease in his outline; but the stiffness of a bust in all his portraits. Thence, though more faithful to a likeness, his heads want air and the softness of flesh, so conspicuous in Rosalba's pictures.

Henry Robert Morland.—Was the pupil of his father, a painter, who lived on the lower side of St. James's Square. He was among the first exhibitors in the year 1760, when the subject of his picture was a "Boy's Head," in crayons, one of the best of his productions. He was rather an unsettled man, frequently changing his residence; but in the latter part of his life he resided in Stephen Street, Rathbone Place, where he died in December, 1797, about seventy-three years of age. Of the children which he left, his eldest son, *George*, was a remarkable example of abilities in art and at the same time of depravity in manners and morals. As an artist, he received his first instructions from his father, but very soon surpassed his master. His early productions were landscapes, and he painted one or two small conversation pieces, but his favourite subjects were animals, chiefly of the domestic kind—horses, dogs, pigs, and other cattle, which he painted in a very masterly manner.

"McArdell" (says Smith in his Life of Nollekens), "resided at the Golden Ball, Henrietta Street, Covent Garden. Of the numerous and splendid productions of this excellent engraver from pictures by Sir Joshua, nothing can be said after the declaration of Reynolds himself, that 'McArdell's prints would immortalize him;' however, I will venture to indulge in one remark more, namely, that that engraver has conferred immortality also upon himself in his wonderful print from Hogarth's picture of Captain Coram, the founder of the *Foundling Hospital.* A brilliant proof of this head in its finest possible state of condition, in my humble opinion, surpasses any thing in mezzotinto now extant."

George Michael Moser.—Born at Schaffhausen in Switzerland. When young, he visited a distant Canton, where he met with one of his townsmen, and being inclined to travel, was soon persuaded to make a tour to England. He and his companion performed the journey together, chiefly through France, riding and walking occasionally, as best suited their convenience and finances. When they arrived in London, the person to whom Mr. Moser had letters of recommendation, introduced him to the notice of Mr. Trotter, at that time a celebrated cabinet-maker and upholsterer, in Soho, by whom he was employed as chaser for the brass decorations of cabinets, tables, and such articles of furniture as required those species of ornaments, which at that time were in fashion. At the foundation of the Royal Academy in 1768, Mr. Moser was appointed the keeper; and when the king was pleased to fix the Institution at Somerset House, he had apartments allotted to him in that ancient palace, where he resided until the present building was finished, when suitable accommodations were allotted to the keeper. This situation Mr. Moser continued to fill, with the greatest respectability, till his death, which happened the 23rd January 1783: and such was the respect which the students entertained for him, that many of them voluntarily attended his funeral. He was interred in the burial-ground of Covent Garden. As an artist, Mr. Moser ranked very high, for his abilities were not confined merely to chasing; he also might be considered as one of our best medalists, as is sufficiently testified by several of his works in that line of art. He likewise painted in enamel with great beauty and accuracy, and many of his productions, particularly some watch-cases, were most elegant and classical in their enrichments. He was well skilled in the construction of the human figure, and, as an instructor in the academy, his manners, as well as his abilities, rendered him a most respectable master to the students.

Jeremiah Meyers.—Born at Tubingen, in the Duchy of Wurtemberg. He came to England when fourteen years old, in company with his father, who was a painter of small subjects, of no great talent. The son pursued miniature painting, and studied under Zincke, who at that time was deservedly esteemed, particularly for his miniatures in enamel; but Meyers surpassed his master in the elegance and gusto of his portraits, a superiority, which he acquired by his attention to the works of Sir Joshua Reynolds, who, as well as himself, was at that time rising to fame. In the year 1761, the Society for the Encouragement of Arts offered a premium of twenty guineas for the best drawing of a profile of the king, for the purpose of having a die engraved from it, and Meyers obtained the prize. He was afterwards appointed miniature painter to the queen. Mr. Meyers was many years a member of the Academy in St. Martin's Lane, and at the institution of the Royal Academy he was chosen one of the members. He long resided in Covent Garden; but at the latter part of his life retired to Kew, where he died the 20th January, 1789, and was buried there.

Gabriel Mathyas.—This gentleman for some years practised as a painter, and, as he himself humourously observed, was at Rome upon his studies long enough to have painted like Raphael; but his talents did not qualify him to attain so elevated a rank in art. In the exhibition of the year 1761, at the Society's Room in the Strand, there were pictures by him; one in particular of a sailor splicing a rope, from which there is a mezzotinto print by McArdell. He continued to exhibit for about two years after, when he ceased to practice the art, and confined his attention to the duties of his situation, as he possessed a respectable appointment in the Office of the Privy Purse. He chiefly resided at Acton, where he died the latter part of the year 1804, at a very advanced age.

Francis Milner Newton.—A portrait painter, the pupil of M. Teuscher. At a time when the artists were accustomed to assemble for their mutual benefit, before they obtained a Charter, Mr. Newton was generally chosen Secretary, and when they were incorporated, he was appointed to the same office. This situation he resigned in consequence of the disputes that took place among the members of that body. At the foundation of the Royal Academy he was chosen a member; he was also appointed the first Secretary to that Institution; and when the buildings at Somerset Place were finished, he had apartments allotted to him where he resided until December, 1788, when, finding the duties of his situation increase beyond his declining powers, he resigned his post, and was succeeded by Mr. Richards. He was for several years Deputy Muster master of England, but quitted that engagement some years before his death.

Robert Edge Pine.—Born in London, was the son of Mr. John Pine, the engraver, who executed and published an elegant edition of Horace, the whole of which is engraved. He chiefly practised as a portrait painter, and was considered among the best colourists of his time. He resided several years in St. Martin's Lane. In the year 1760, he produced a picture as candidate for the premium then offered by the Society for the Encouragement of Arts, &c. for the best historical picture painted in oil colours; the figures to be as large as life, and the subject to be taken from English history. Mr. Pine selected "the Surrender of Calais," and obtained the first prize of one hundred guineas.

RAVENET.—Was employed to engrave copper-plates from which the articles were stamped, consisting of scrolls, foliage, shells, pastoral subjects, and figures of every description.

REIBENSTEIN.—Was a native either of Holland or Germany, but resided in England several years. He chiefly painted draperies, sometimes portraits in oil. In the catalogues of the first and second exhibitions, his name is to be found as an exhibitor; the subjects of the pictures are—"Dead Game and Still Life." He was for some years a member of the Academy in St. Martin's Lane. He died about the year 1763.

NICHOLAS REVETT, younger son of Andrew Revett, Esq. of Brandeston Hall, Suffolk, was by profession an architect; and it was from him that Mr. Stuart first caught his ideas of that science, in which (quitting the painter's art) he afterwards made so conspicuous a figure. Their acquaintance first began at Rome; whence they travelled to Athens, for the purpose of investigating the remains of ancient grandeur still to be found in the ruins of that celebrated metropolis. Mr. Revett also travelled through Asia Minor with Dr. Chandler, and published the Ionian Antiquities, being engaged for that purpose by the Dilettante Society. At the distance of forty years, at the request of Sir Lionel Lyde, Bart., of Ayott St. Lawrence, Herts, Mr. Revett added another trophy to his architectural fame. The old church, at the back of Sir Lionel's mansion-house being dilapidated, though not incapable of restoration at a far less expense, it was determined to erect a new one fronting the house, at the western extremity of the park, in a style of architecture not confined to any one Grecian model. After the new church had been consecrated, and made use of, Bishop Thurlow refused his license to take down the old one, which still remains, with the monuments of its patrons and benefactors, a beautiful ruin. Mr. Revett, who was described in 1789, as "occasionally enlivening a small select circle of friends with his lively conversation," died at a very advanced age, in June 1804. The effects of his labours and researches will for ever remain monuments of his memory and talents as an artist, whilst those noble publications of Palmyra, Balbeck, and the Ionian Antiquities, are admitted into the cabinets of the curious. His valuable library of books of Architecture and Drawings by himself and others, including many on sacred subjects in four volumes by Dr. Stukeley, was sold by Mr. Christie.—*Literary Anecdotes.*

PAUL SANDBY.—Was born at Nottingham, 1732. In 1746, he came to London, and having an early predilection for the arts, procured admission into the Drawing-room of the Tower, where he first studied. He was a draughtsman of great eminence and was employed on public surveys. On the institution of the Royal Academy, he was elected a Royal Academician. He died in 1809, in the 77th year of his age. He is said to have contributed much to the reputation of the English School of landscape painting. His paintings in water colours are highly esteemed.

JARVIS SPENCER.—A miniature painter of much celebrity. He was originally a gentleman's servant, but having a natural turn to the pursuits of art, amused himself with drawing. It happened that some one of the family with whom he lived sat for their portrait to a miniature-painter, and when the work was completed, it was shewn to him; upon which he observed, that he thought he could copy it. This hint was received with much surprise, but he was indulged with permission to make the attempt, and his success was such, that he not only gave perfect satisfaction, but also acquired the encouragement and patronage of those he served, and, by their interest, became a fashionable painter of the day.

LUKE SULLIVAN.—A native of Ireland, lodged at the White Bear, Piccadilly. "I believe," (says Smith), "nothing has ever surpassed his etching of 'the March to Finchley,' from Hogarth's picture in the *Foundling Hospital.* It is full of the painter's effect, and though only an etching, every part is perfectly made out; and I most heartily wish, fine as the finished plate unquestionably is, that Hogarth had published it in its earliest state. Of this beautiful etching I have an impression under my care in the British Museum. Luke Sullivan was also a most exquisite miniature-painter, particularly of females. He was a handsome lively fellow; but being too much attached to what are denominated the good things of this world, he died in a miserable state of disease and poverty."

STRANGE.—"The following anecdote of Sir Robert Strange," (says Smith), "was related to me by the late Richard Cooper, who instructed Queen Charlotte in drawing, and was for some time drawing master to Eton school. I shall endeavour to relate it as nearly as possible in his own words. 'Robert Strange,' said he, 'was a countryman of mine, a North Briton, who served his time to my father as an engraver, and was a soldier in the rebel army of 1745. It so happened, when Duke William put them to flight, that Strange, finding a door open, made his way into the house,—ascended to the first floor, and entered a room where a young lady was seated: she was at her needlework and singing. Young Strange implored her protection. The lady, without rising or being the least disconcerted, desired him to get under her hoop. He immediately stooped, and the amiable woman covered him up. Shortly after this, the house was searched; the lady continued at her work singing as before, and the soldiers, upon entering the room, considering Miss Lumsdale alone, respectfully retired. Robert, as soon as the search was over, being released from his covering, kissed the hand of his protectress, at which moment, for the first time, he found himself in love. He married the lady; and no persons, beset as they were with early difficulties, lived more happily.' Strange afterwards became a loyal man, though for a length of time he sighed to be pardoned by his king; who, however, was graciously pleased to be reconciled to him and afterwards knighted him. No man was more incessant in his application, or fonder of his art than Sir Robert Strange; nor could any publisher boast of more integrity as to his mode of delivering subscription impressions. He never took off more proofs than were really bespoken, and every name was put upon the print as it came out of the press, unless it were faulty, and then it was destroyed; not laid aside for future sale, as has been the practice with some of our late publishers. Sir Robert Strange was born in 1721, and died in 1792."

Samuel Scott.—Was not only the first painter of his own age, but one whose works will charm in *every* age. If he was but second to Vandevelde in sea-pieces, he excelled him in variety, and often introduced buildings in his pictures with consummate skill. His views of London Bridge, of the Quay at the Custom House, &c. were equal to his Marines, and his figures were judiciously chosen and admirably painted; nor were his washed drawings inferior to his finished pictures. The gout harassed and terminated his life; but he had formed a pupil who compensated for his loss to the public, Mr. Marlow. Mr. Scott died 12th of October, 1772, leaving an only daughter by his wife, who survived him till April, 1781.—*Walpole.*

Michael Henry Spang.—Was a Dane, who drew the figure beautifully and with anatomical truth; a most essential component of the art, indispensably requisite for all those who would climb to the summit of fame. Spang produced the small anatomical figure so well known to every draughtsman who assiduously studies his art. He also designed and executed the figures on the pediment of Earl Spencer's house in the Green Park, and the decorations on the screen at the Admiralty.—*Smith.*

Peter Toms.—Was son of Mr. Toms, the engraver, and a pupil of Hudson, and might be considered as a portrait painter, but his chief excellence was in painting draperies. In that branch of the art, so useful to a fashionable face-painter, he was much employed, first by Sir Joshua Reynolds, and afterwards by Cotes; he also executed some for Mr. West. Among the pictures which he did for Sir Joshua, are some very excellent; and candour must allow, that many of Sir Joshua's best whole-lengths are those to which Toms painted the draperies; among them was the picture of Lady Elizabeth Keppell, in the dress she wore as bride-maid to the Queen; for which he was paid twelve guineas, a very slender price in proportion to the merit of the piece: but Sir Joshua was not remarkably liberal upon these occasions, of which circumstance Mr. Toms did not neglect to complain. When the Royal Academy was founded, he was chosen one of the members. He had also an appointment in the Herald's College.

John Williams.—A portrait-painter, said to have been a pupil of Richardson. His name stands in the first exhibition catalogue to a half-length portrait of Mr. Beard, the celebrated singer, from which there is a mezzotinto print by McArdell. This painter was very superior in abilities to many of his cotemporary artists, as was evinced by a three-quarter portrait, exhibited at the Society's Rooms in the Strand, 1761, which was much and deservedly admired.

Benjamin Wilson.—A native of Yorkshire. His father was in the clothing trade at Leeds, who, meeting with misfortunes, was not able to give his son much assistance. When young he was sent to London, recommended to Dr. Berdmore, master of the Charterhouse, who patronized him. It is not known whether he received any regular education as an artist; but, by his natural talents and steady application, he acquired very considerable abilities as a portrait-painter, and may be truly said to have assisted much in improving the manner of portraiture. He endeavoured to introduce a better style of *chiaro scuro* into his pictures, and the colouring of his heads had more of warmth and nature than the general class of his cotemporary artists could infuse into their works.

Westfield Webb.—A painter of portraits, who resided chiefly in St. Martin's Lane. In the exhibition of 1762, there was a whole-length portrait of Miss Brent, a celebrated singer of that time, painted by this artist. He continued to exhibit until the year 1772, about which time he died. His works are various in their subjects, sometimes landscapes, at other times flowers.

Ware.—A thin sickly little boy, a chimney-sweeper, was amusing himself one morning by drawing, with a piece of chalk, the street front of Whitehall, upon the basement stones of the building itself, carrying his delineations as far as his little arms could possibly reach; and this he was accomplishing by occasionally running into the middle of the street, to look up at the noble edifice, and then returning to the base of the building to proceed with his elevation. It happened that his operations caught the eye of a gentleman of considerable taste and fortune, as he was riding by. He checked the carriage, and after a few minutes observation, called to the boy to come to him, who, upon being asked where he lived, immediately burst into tears, and begged of the gentleman not to tell his master, assuring him he would wipe it all off. "Don't be alarmed," answered the gentleman, at the same time throwing him a shilling, to convince him he intended him no harm. This boy was young Ware. His benefactor then went instantly to his master, in Charles Court, in the

Strand, who gave the boy a most excellent character, at the same time declaring him to be of little use to him, in consequence of his natural bodily weakness. He said he was fully aware of his fondness for chalking, and showed his visitor what a state his walls were in, from the young artist having drawn the portico of St. Martin's Church upon them, in various places. The gentleman purchased the remainder of the boy's time, gave him an excellent education, then sent him to Italy, and upon his return, employed him, and introduced him to his friends as an architect.—*Smith.*

JOSEPH WILTON.—Was born in London, July 16th, 1722. He was the son of a plasterer, who, by a vast increase of income, arising principally from a manufactory, in imitation of that in France, which he established for making the papier-machie ornaments for chimney-pieces, and frames for looking-glasses, was enabled to rebuild his premises on the south-west corner of Hedge Lane, Charing Cross. Joseph, having a strong natural inclination to become a sculptor, was taken by his father to Nivelle, in Brabant, to study under Lament Delvaux, an artist, who had for several years resided in London. From Nivelle, in 1744, he went to Paris, where he assiduously studied in the academy directed by the famous sculptor, Pigalle, so warmly patronized by Voltaire, of whom Pigalle made a truly spirited bust. In 1747, after gaining the silver medal, and having acquired the power of cutting marble, he, accompanied by Roubilliac, the sculptor, went to Rome, where, in 1750, he not only had the honour of receiving the jubilee gold medal, engraved by Hamerani, given by Pope Benedict XIV., but acquired the patronage of William Locke, Esq.

Francis Zuccarelli.—A native of Florence. In the early part of his life he studied as an historical painter, but afterwards confined his practice to the painting of landscape, with small figures, in which he acquired a very beautiful manner both of composing and executing his pictures. At the foundation of the Royal Academy, he was chosen a member. About the year 1759, he painted a set of designs for tapestries, which were executed in the manufactory of Paul Saunders, the upholsterer, who at that time possessed a patent as tapestry weaver to his Majesty. They were wrought for the late Earl of Egremont, to decorate some part of the house which he built in Piccadilly.

Christian Frederick Zincke.—Was born at Dresden about 1684, and came to England in 1706, where he studied under Boit, whom, at length, he not only surpassed, but rivalled Petitot. "I have," (says Walpole,) "a head of Cowley, by him, after Sir Peter Lely, which is allowed to excel any single work of that charming enameller. The impassioned glow of sentiment, the eyes swimming with youth and tenderness, and the natural fall of the long ringlets that flow round the unbuttoned collar, are rendered with the most exquisite nature, and finished with elaborate care." For a great number of years Mr. Zincke had as much business as he could exe-

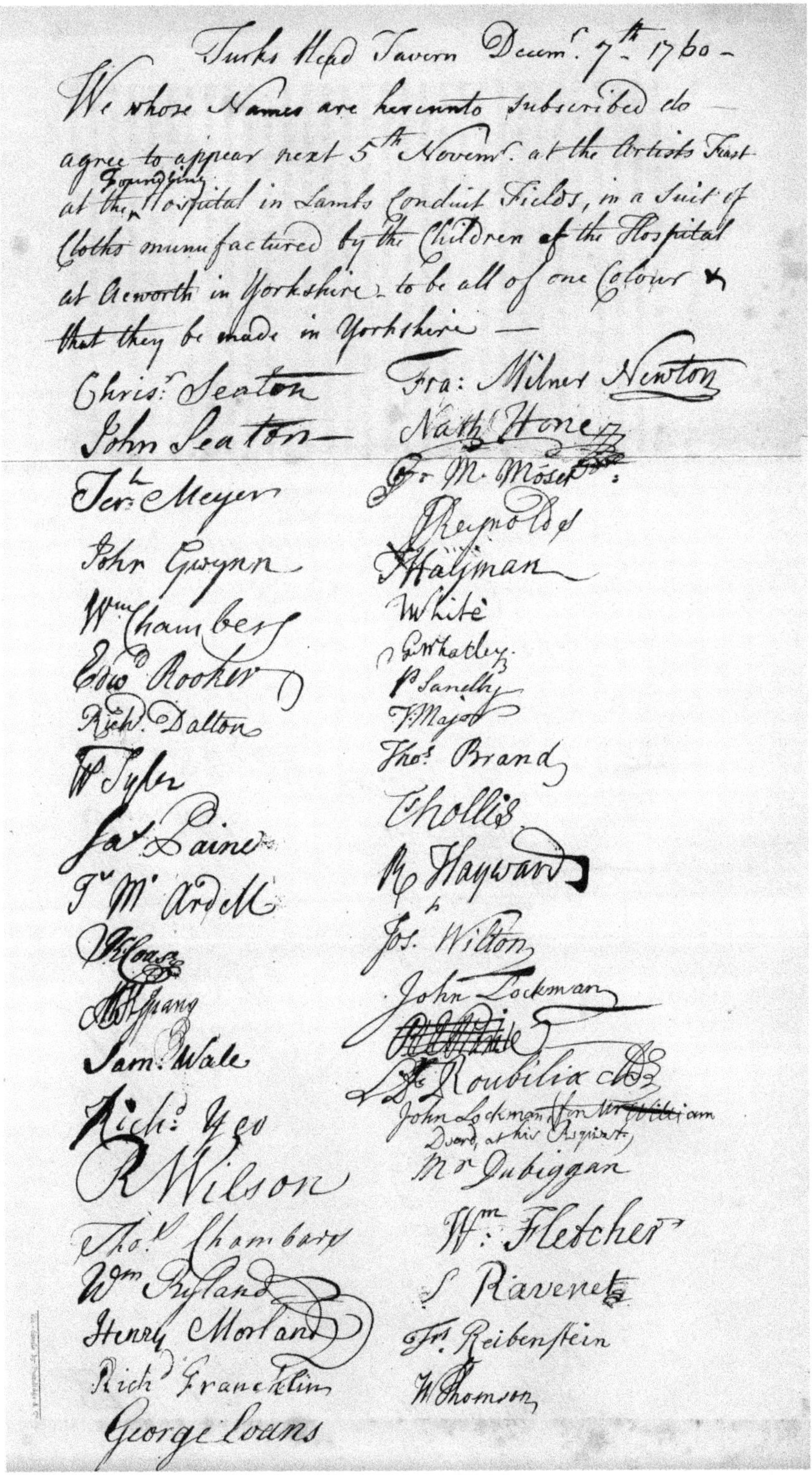

Turks Head Tavern Decem^r. 7th 1760 –

We whose Names are hereunto subscribed do – agree to appear next 5th Novem^r. at the Artists Feast at the Foundling Hospital in Lambs Conduit Fields, in a Suit of Cloths manufactured by the Children of the Hospital at Acworth in Yorkshire – to be all of one Colour & that they be made in Yorkshire –

Chris^r. Seaton
John Seaton
Jer^h. Meyer
John Gwynn
W^m. Chambers
Edwd. Rooker
Rich^d. Dalton
W. Tyler
Ja^s. Paine
J^s. M^c.Ardell
[illegible]
[illegible]
Saml. Wale
Rich^d. Yeo
R Wilson
Thos. Chambers
W^m. Ryland
Henry Morland
Rich^d. Francklin
George Evans

Fra: Milner Newton
Nathl. Hone
G. M. Moser
J Reynolds
F Hayman
White
G Whatley
P Sandby
T. Major
Thos. Brand
T Hollis
R Hayward
Jos. Wilton
John Lockman
[illegible]
L. F. Roubiliac
John Lockman for M^r. William Doord, at his Request.
M^r. Dubiggan
W^m. Fletcher
S Ravenet
Fr^s. Reibenstein
W Thomson

The material originally positioned here is too large for reproduction in this reissue. A PDF can be downloaded from the web address given on page iv of this book, by clicking on 'Resources Available'.

cute; and when, at last, he raised his price from twenty to thirty guineas, it was occasioned by a desire of lessening his fatigue; for no man, so superior in his profession, was less intoxicated with vanity.

In the year 1760 the Hospital, being then under the patronage of Parliament, who contributed large sums of money upon condition that all children tendered for admission should be received, had grown to such an extent as to embrace within its arms several thousands of Children, so that the Governors were obliged to open Branch Establishments in the Country to receive them. One of these establishments was at Ackworth, in Yorkshire. At this place the children were usefully employed in the manufacture of cloth. This led some of the artists to the benevolent and enthusiastic idea of promoting the good of the Charity by appearing at their Festival in 1761, in clothing made by these children.

The curious document annexed is confirmatory of this interesting circumstance, and as evidence of the earnestness of the artists in this step, there is extant a letter dated 15th December, 1760, from the Rev. Dr. Lee, the indefatigable Governor of the Hospital at Ackworth, in which he says to the Treasurer in London, "Mr. Paine has wrote about clothing for the artists of the Turk's Head Club, and I should be glad to know if the twenty you speak of are not the same he writes about, and says will be in number sixty in a little time. He writes in the name of those gentlemen who will honour us with an uniform against their next Annual Meeting. I am to send him patterns of colours, but hope he'll choose that of your coat or something near it, because the deep coppers, from the nature of the dye, render the wool too tender for the spinning of our young artists to make any moderate profit. Of this you'll please to give him a hint, as it may not be so proper to insert it in my letter to him, which probably he will show to his brethren."

At what precise period these meetings of the artists at the Hospital ceased is not known, but there is no doubt that as the Royal Academy, which was founded in 1768, became established and consolidated, the convivial presence of its members was transferred to a more appropriate arena. The "Gentleman's Magazine," of the 5th November, 1763, thus testifies that up to that period the meetings were still continued.

"The Artists of London and Westminster held their Anniversary at the Foundling Hospital in commemoration of the day, and were entertained by the Children with an Anthem. A blind boy performed on the organ, and a little girl of five years of age the solo part of the vocal music."

Charles Lamb, in one of his critical essays, remarks that Hogarth seemed to take particular delight in introducing *Children* into his works.

As evidence that this characteristic was not the mere ideality of a painter, but emanated from that

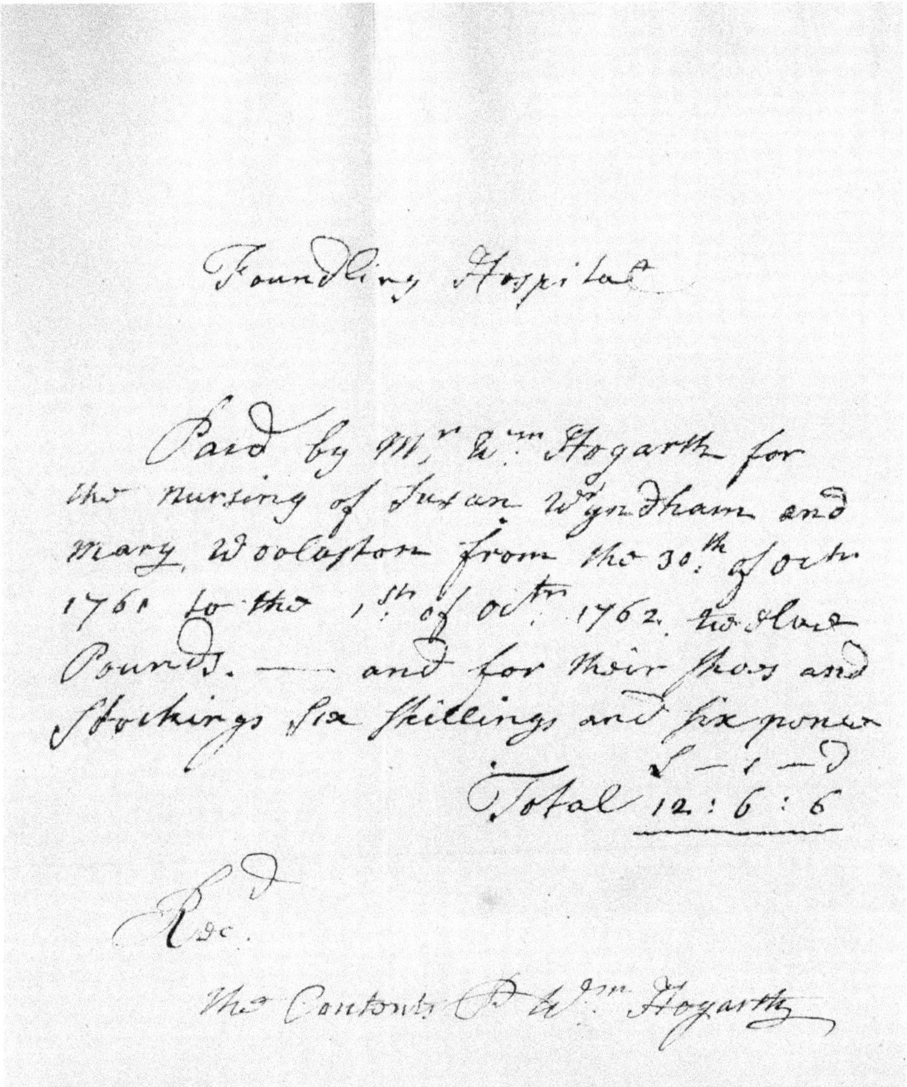

Foundling Hospital

Paid by Mr. Wm. Hogarth for the nursing of Susan Wyndham and Mary Woolaston from the 30th of Octr. 1761 to the 1st of Octr. 1762 twelve Pounds. —— and for their shoes and Stockings six shillings and six pence

£ – s – d

Total 12 : 6 : 6

Recd.

the Contents ℗ Wm. Hogarth

Fac Simile by Standidge & Co.

The material originally positioned here is too large for reproduction in this reissue. A PDF can be downloaded from the web address given on page iv of this book, by clicking on 'Resources Available'.

generous heart which guided his actions, the following anecdote of this extraordinary man is recorded.

It was the practice at this period, of the Hospital (as indeed it is at the present time), to nurse the *Infant* Children of the establishment in the Country till about five years of age, by distributing them amongst cottagers in certain districts, superintended by competent authorities in the neighbourhood.

These authorities formerly performed their interesting office *gratuitously*, and they consisted of resident gentry or ladies. In or about the year 1760, the Governors at the request of Hogarth, sent several of these poor infants to Chiswick, where the painter resided, he engaging, along with Mrs. Hogarth, to see them properly taken care of. The annexed is a copy of his Bill for the Maintenance, &c. of two of these children, who were returned to the Hospital by Mrs. Hogarth at her husband's death in 1764. It is impossible to revert to the life of Hogarth, so full of labour in his art, and at the latter period of his existence, so charged with vexation and controversy, by reason of the defection and abuse of his quondam friends, Wilkes and Churchill, without feeling some degree of admiration for one who, amidst all this, should be found engaged in so humble a charity as that of watching over the destiny of parentless and helpless foundlings.

Charity has the peculiar charm of engaging, for her attendants, men of all kinds of political sentiments, but even she is not free from the consequences of *private* enmity or animosity. This was evidenced by the quarrel between Wilkes* and Hogarth. They were both associated in the same work of benevolence at the Foundling Hospital, meeting at the same board as Governors, but no sooner did a personal quarrel arise between them, than they ceased to attend in their places, as if each was afraid of meeting the other, even within the walls of Charity herself.

"Before the birth of Hogarth," says Cunningham, "there are many centuries in which we relied wholly on foreign skill. With him and after him arose a succession of eminent painters, who have spread the fame of British Art far and wide."

Of many of those who arose with him, and of a few that followed after, some further account will be found in the following pages.

* The Governors had a Branch Hospital at Aylesbury (for which place Wilkes was returned toParliament), and they appointed him the Treasurer of that Hospital. When he left the Kingdom in 1764, some ugly disclosures connected with the Accounts took place, by no means creditable to "honest John."

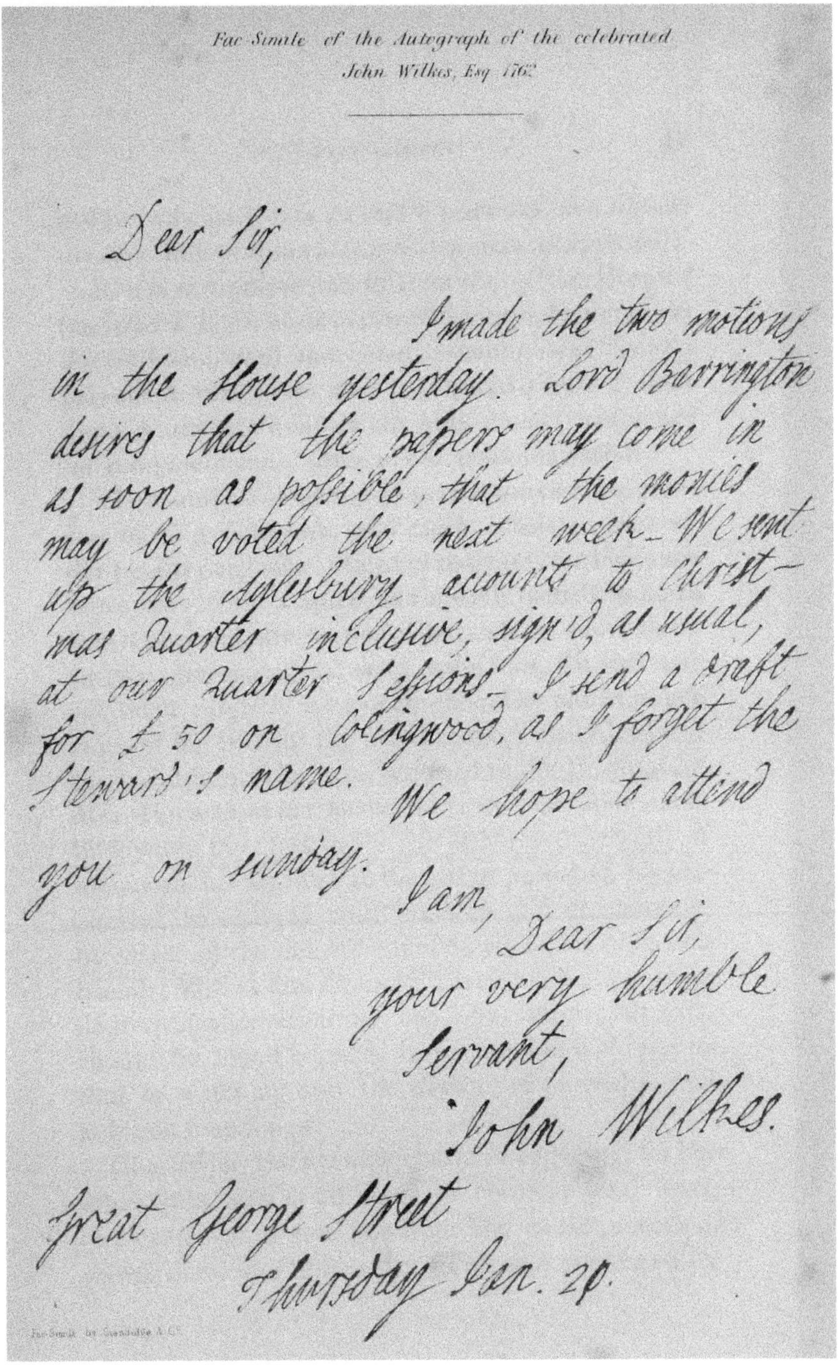

Fac-Simile of the Autograph of the celebrated
John Wilkes, Esq 1762

Dear Sir,

I made the two motions in the House yesterday. Lord Barrington desires that the papers may come in as soon as possible, that the monies may be voted the next week. We sent up the Aylesbury accounts to Christmas Quarter inclusive, sign'd, as usual, at our Quarter Sessions. I send a draft for £ 50 on Colingwood, as I forget the Steward's name. We hope to attend you on sunday.

I am,
Dear Sir,
your very humble
Servant,
John Wilkes.

Great George Street
Thursday Jan. 20.

Fac-Simile by Standidge & Co.

The material originally positioned here is too large for reproduction in this reissue. A PDF can be downloaded from the web address given on page iv of this book, by clicking on 'Resources Available'.

CATALOGUE OF PICTURES, &c.

AT THE

FOUNDLING HOSPITAL.

THE COURT ROOM.

The subject of the first large picture in this room is that of

HAGAR AND ISHMAEL.

"*And the angel of the Lord called to Hagar out of heaven, and said to her, What aileth thee, Hagar? Fear not, for God hath heard the voice of the lad where he is.*"

By HIGHMORE.

"Joseph Highmore," (says Walpole,) "was bred a lawyer, but quitted that profession for painting, which he exercised with reputation amongst the successors of Kneller, under whom he entered into an academy, and living at first in the city, was much employed there for family pieces. He afterwards removed to Lincoln's-inn-fields, and painted the portraits of the Knights of the Bath, on the revival of that order, for the series of plates, which he first projected, and which were engraved by Pine. Highmore published two pamphlets, one called 'A Critical Examination of the Ceiling, painted by Rubens, in the Banqueting House,' in which architecture is introduced, as far as relates to perspective, together with the discussion of a question which has been the subject of debate amongst painters; written many years since, but now first published, 1764. The other 'The Practice of Perspective, on the principles of Dr. Brook Taylor, &c.'; written many years since, but now first published, 1764; quarto, with fifty copper plates. He had a daughter, who was married to a prebendary of Canterbury, and to her he retired on his quitting business, and died there in March, 1780, aged 88."

No. 2.

LITTLE CHILDREN BROUGHT TO CHRIST.

" Jesus said, Suffer little children to come unto me and forbid them not, for of such is the kingdom of heaven."

By JAMES WILLS.

Mr. James Wills was a portrait-painter, and he also painted some historical subjects, but not meeting with much success in his profession he quitted it, and, having received a liberal education, took orders. He was for several years Curate of Canons, in Middlesex, and at the death of the incumbent, Mr. Hallett gave him the living, which he enjoyed till his death. He died in the latter part of the year 1777. His name stands in the first exhibition catalogue to an historical subject, "Liberality and Modesty." He was also an exhibitor the following year, but his name is there inserted without any clerical distinction, he therefore at that time had not taken orders. In the year 1768, he was appointed chaplain to the chartered society of artists, with a salary of thirty pounds a year. He preached one sermon (the text of which was taken from Job, Chap. xxxvii. verse 14.—Stand still, and consider the wondrous works of God,) at Covent Garden Church, on St. Luke's Day, in the same year. This discourse was afterwards printed at the request of the society, but he did not long enjoy his appointment, in consequence of the disputes which broke out among the members of that body. In the early part of his life he translated Fresnoys's Art of Painting.

No. 3.

THE FINDING OF THE INFANT MOSES IN THE BULL-RUSHES.

"*And the maid went and called the child's mother. And Pharoah's daughter said unto her, take this child and nurse it for me, and I will give thee thy wages.*"

By FRANCIS HAYMAN, R.A.

This painter was born in or near Exeter, and was the pupil of Brown. In the early part of his life, he was much employed by Fleetwood, the proprietor of Drury Lane Theatre, for whom he painted many scenes. In the pursuit of his profession, he was not extremely assiduous, being more convivial than studious, yet he acquired a very considerable degree of power in his art, and was unquestionably the best historical painter in the kingdom, before the arrival of Cipriani. It was this superiority of talent that introduced him to the notice of Mr. Jonathan Tiers, the founder and proprietor of Vauxhall, by whom he was much employed in decorating the gardens of that place. Walpole says, that the aforementioned works recommended him to much practice in making designs for books; the truth is, that his reputation as an artist was at that time very considerable, and this circumstance led the booksellers to employ him much in making drawings for the prints with which they chose to decorate their publications. When the artists were incorporated by charter, Lambert was appointed first President, but he dying shortly after, Hayman was chosen in his stead, in which office he remained till 1768, when, owing to the proceedings of the majority of the members of the Society he was no longer continued in that station. For this exclusion he was amply recompensed by the immediate foundation of the Royal Academy, of which he was chosen a member, and soon after appointed the librarian. This place he held till his death, which happened on February 2nd, 1776, in the 68th year of his age.

No. 4.

MOSES BROUGHT TO PHAROAH'S DAUGHTER.

"*And the child grew, and she brought him unto Pharoah's daughter, and he became her son. And she called his name Moses.*"

BY HOGARTH.

"The subject of this picture," says Nichols, "is taken at the point of time when the child's mother, whom the princess considers as merely its nurse, has brought him to his patroness, and is receiving from the treasurer the wages of her services.

"The little foundling naturally clings to his nurse, though invited to leave her by the daughter of a monarch; and the eyes of an attendant and a whispering Ethiopian, convey an oblique suspicion that the child has a nearer affinity to their mistress than she chooses to acknowledge.

"On the merits of this painting, two excellent critics have recorded very opposite opinions.

"Mr. John Ireland, who well understood the subject on which he treats, but had weighty reasons for bestowing praise on Hogarth, rather than censure, observes that, considered as a whole, this picture has a more historic air than we often find in the works of Hogarth. The royal Egyptian is graceful, and, in some degree, elevated; the treasurer is marked with austere dignity, and the jewess and child with nature. The scene is superb, and the distant prospect of pyramids, &c. highly picturesque and appropriate to the country. To exhibit this scene, the artist has placed the group at such a distance as to crowd the corners, and leave the centre unoccupied. As the Greeks are said to have received the rudiments of art from Egypt, the line of beauty on the base of a pillar is properly introduced. A crocodile creeping from under the stately chair, may be intended to mark the neighbourhood of the Nile, but is a poor and forced conceit.

"Mr. Stevens, whose discriminating taste is indisputable, but who scrutinized the works of Hogarth with an asperity somewhat too severe, says, 'The daughter of the Egyptian monarch appears to more advantage in the print than on the canvass; and the colouring is beneath criticism.'

"I have been told that the head of Pharaoh's daughter was copied from one Seaton. Hogarth could not, like Guido, draw a Venus from a common porter."

On each side of these large pictures are smaller ones, of a circular form, representing the principal Hospitals of the day, viz.—

GREENWICH HOSPITAL.—CHRIST'S HOSPITAL.—
ST. THOMAS'S HOSPITAL.

BY SAMUEL WALE, R.A.

Wale was born in London, and brought up as an engraver of plate; he afterwards studied design in the academy of St. Martin's Lane. He also practised painting, in which he imitated the manner of

Hayman, and executed several decorative pieces for ceilings: but his chief employment was among the booksellers, for whom he made many designs, the principal part of which were engraved by Mr. Grignion. He understood architecture and perspective, and greatly assisted Mr. Gwynn in the decorations of his architectural drawings, particularly in the section of St. Paul's, and was of service to him in the literary part of his publications. At the establishment of the Royal Academy, Wale was chosen one of the members, and appointed the first professor of perspective in that institution. Upon the death of Mr. R. Wilson, he was also made librarian, both of which places he held till his death, which was on the 6th of February, 1786. For many years before his death, he was so infirm as not to be able to read his lectures in the academy, and was therefore permitted to give private instructions to the students at his own house.

CHELSEA AND BETHLEM HOSPITALS.

By HAYTLEY.

This painter, who has considerable merit, and obtained some distinction amongst his brethren, is without a biographer, so that the particulars of his life and the date of his death are unknown. He was, however, made a governor of the Foundling Hospital in 1746, for his artistical donations, and was present at the festivals held annually by the artists in that establishment.

THE CHARTERHOUSE.

By THOMAS GAINSBOROUGH, R.A.

This excellent artist was born in 1727, at Sudbury, in Suffolk. His father was a clothier in that town, and Thomas was the youngest of three sons. At a proper age he was sent to London, and placed under the tuition of Hayman, with whom he, however, stayed but a short time. After quitting his master, he for some time resided in Hatton Garden, and practised painting of portraits of a small size, and also pursued his favourite subject, landscape. After residing a short time in London, he married a young lady who possessed an annuity of two hundred pounds, and then retired to Ipswich, in Suffolk. From Ipswich Gainsborough removed to Bath, where he settled about the year 1758, and began his career as a portrait-painter, at the low price of five guineas for a three-quarter canvas: however, his great facility in producing a likeness, increased his employment and fame, and he soon raised his price from five to eight guineas. At Bath he resided several years, occasionally sending his works to the exhibition in London, which he did, for the first time in 1761. In 1774, he quitted Bath, and settled in London, in a part of the large house in Pall Mall, which was originally built by the Duke de Schomberg. In this respectable situation, possessed of fame, and in the acquisition of fortune, he was disturbed by a complaint in his neck, which was not much noticed upon the first attack, nor was it apprehended to be more than a swelling in the glands of the throat, which it was expected would subside in a short time; but it was soon discovered to be a cancer, which baffled the skill of the first medical professors. Finding the danger of his situation, he settled his affairs, and composed himself to meet the fatal moment, and calmly expired on the 2nd of August, 1788, in the sixty-first year of his age, and was buried, according to his own request, near the remains of his former friend, Mr. Kirby, in Kew Churchyard. His funeral was attended by Sir J. Reynolds, Sir William Chambers, Mr. P. Sandby, Mr. West, Mr. Bartolozzi, and Mr. Samuel Cotes.

ST. GEORGE'S HOSPITAL, AND FOUNDLING HOSPITAL.

By RICHARD WILSON, R.A.

This eminent artist, it is believed, was born in Montgomeryshire, where his father, a clergyman, possessed a small benefice, but was afterwards collated to the living of Mould, in Flintshire, while the son was very young. His connections were highly respectable, being maternally related to the Lord Chancellor Camden, who acknowledged him as his cousin. At the time of life when it was necessary to fix on some profession, young Wilson was sent to London and placed under the tuition of T. Wright, a portrait-painter of very slender abilities. Wilson, however, acquired so much knowledge from his master, as to become a painter of portraits equal to most of his contemporaries. He must also have acquired a degree of rank in his profession; for about the year 1749, he painted a large picture of George the Third (then Prince of Wales), with his brother the Duke of York, for Dr. Hayter, Bishop of Norwich, at that time tutor to the princes. After having practised some years in London, he went to Italy, and was at Rome at the same time with several English artists, who afterwards became the ornaments of their country. In Italy he continued to study portrait-painting, though not with the same success as attended Sir Joshua Reynolds; for he was then unacquainted with the peculiar bias of his talents, and might probably have remained long ignorant of his latent powers, but for the following accident:—

While Wilson was at Venice, he painted a small landscape, which, being seen by Zuccarelli, that artist was so much struck with the merit of the piece, that he strongly urged Wilson to pursue that branch of the art, which advice Wilson followed, and became one of the first landscape painters in Europe. His studies in landscape must have been attended with rapid success, for he had some pupils in that line of art while at Rome, and his works were so much esteemed, that Mengo painted his portrait, for which Wilson, in return, painted a landscape.

It is not known at what time he returned to England, but he was in London in 1758, and resided over the north arcade of the Piazza, Covent Garden, at which time he had obtained great celebrity as a landscape painter.

To the first exhibition of 1760, he sent his picture of Niobe, which confirmed his reputation.

In 1765, he exhibited (with other pictures) a view of Rome from the Villa Madama, which was purchased by the then Marquis of Tavistock.

Though he had acquired great fame, yet he did not find that constant employment which his abilities deserved. This neglect might probably result from his own conduct, for it must be confessed that Wilson was not very attentive to his interest; and though a man of strong sense and superior education to most of the artists of his time, he did not possess that suavity of manners which distinguished many of his contemporaries. On this account his connections and employment insensibly diminished, and left him in the latter part of his life in comfortless infirmity. When the Royal Academy was instituted, he was chosen one of the members, and after the death of Hayman, made the librarian, which situation he retained until his decayed health compelled him to retire into Wales, where he died in May, 1782, aged sixty-eight.

Over the mantle-piece of the Court-room is a beautiful basso-relievo,

By RYSBRACK,

representing children engaged in navigation and husbandry, being the employments to which the children of the Hospital were supposed to be destined.

John Michael Rysbrack, was born at Brussels, and was the son of a landscape-painter. He studied under Theodore Balant, a famous sculptor; came to England in 1720, and resided in Vere Street, Oxford Street, where he had extensive workshops, which his great run of business required. On these premises he died, and was buried in Marylebone Churchyard, 11th January, 1770. After his decease, there were sales by auction held at his house, in one of which was an immense number of his own drawings mounted with uniform borders, executed in bister; and some of the most excellent of them are still to be found in the portfolios of collectors. Rysbrack executed many busts for noblemen and others, and was much employed on mural and other monuments.

The side table, of Grecian marble, is supported by carved figures in wood, representing children playing with a goat, and was presented by Mr. John Sanderson (architect), who was employed with others in the erection of the Hospital.

There are also two fine busts, casts from the Antique, one of Caracalla and the other of Marcus Aurelius. They were given by Mr. Richard Dalton, who held several important offices connected with the arts, and was sent to Italy by George III. to collect articles of *vertu* to enrich His Majesty's collection.

The ornamented ceiling was done by Mr. Wilton, the father of the eminent sculptor.

COMMITTEE ROOM.

THE MARCH TO FINCHLEY.

By HOGARTH.

The following is considered the most authentic account of this celebrated picture, and is from the pen of Mr. Justice Welsh, the intimate friend and companion of Hogarth.

"The scene of this representation is laid at Tottenham Court Turnpike; the King's Head, Adam and Eve, and the turnpike house, in full view; beyond which are discovered, parties of the guards, baggage, &c. marching towards Highgate, and a beautiful distant prospect of the country; the sky finely painted. The picture, considered together, affords a view of a military march, and the humours and disorders consequent thereupon. Near the centre of the picture, the painter has exhibited his principal figure, which is a handsome young grenadier, in whose face is strongly depicted repentance mixed with pity and concern; the occasion of which is disclosed by two females putting in their claim for his person, one of whom has hold of his right arm, and the other has *seized* his left. The figure upon his right hand, and perhaps placed there by the painter by way of preference, as the object of love is more desirable than that of duty, is a fine young girl in her person, debauched, with child, and reduced to the miserable employ of selling ballads, and who, with a look full of love, tenderness, and distress, casts up her eyes upon her undoer, and with tears descending down her cheeks, seems to say, 'sure you cannot—will not leave me!' The person and deportment of this figure well justifies the painters's turning the body of the youth towards her. The woman upon the left is a strong contrast to this girl; for rage and jealousy have thrown the human countenance into no amiable or desirable form. This is the wife of the youth, who, finding him engaged with such an *ugly slut*, assaults him with a violence natural to a woman whose person and beauty are neglected. Added to the fury of her countenance, and the dreadful weapon her tongue, another terror appears in her hand, equally formidable, which is a roll of papers, whereon is written 'The Remembrancer;' a word of dire and triple import; for while it shows the occupation the *amiable bearer* is engaged in, it reminds the youth of an unfortunate circumstance he would gladly forget; and the same word is also a cant expression, to signify the blow she is meditating. And here, I value myself upon hitting the true meaning, and entering into the spirit of the great author of that celebrated Journal called, 'The Remembrancer.'

"It is easily discernible that the two females are of different parties. The ballad of 'God save our noble King,' and a print of 'the Duke of Cumberland,' in the basket of the girl, and the cross upon the back of the wife, with the implements of her occupation, sufficiently denote the painter's intention; and what is truly beautiful, these incidents are applicable to the march. The hard-favoured serjeant directly behind, who enjoys the foregoing scene, is not only a good contrast to the youth, but also, with other helps, throws forward the principal figure. Upon the right of the grenadier is a drummer, who also has his *two remembrancers*, a woman and a boy, the produce of their kinder hours; and who have laid their claim by a violent seizure upon his person. The figure of the woman is that of a complainant, who reminds him of her great application, as well in sending him clean to guard, as other kind offices done, and his promises to make her an honest woman, which he, base and ungrateful, has forgot, and pays her affection with neglect. The craning of her neck shows her remonstrances to be of the shrill kind, in which she is aided by the howling of her boy. The drummer, who has a mixture of fun and wickedness in his face, having heard as many reproaches as suit his present inclinations, with a bite of his lip and a leering eye, applies to the instrument of noise in his profession, and endeavours to drown the united clamour, in which he is luckily aided by the *ear-piercing fife* near him.

"Between the figures before described, but more back in the picture, appears the important but meagre phiz of a Frenchman, in close whisper with an Independent. The first I suppose a spy upon the motion of the army; the other probably drawn into the crowd, in order to give intelligence to his brethren, at their next meeting, to commemorate their noble struggle in support of independence. The

Frenchman exhibits a letter, which he assures him contains positive intelligence that 10,000 of his countrymen are landed in England in support of liberty and independence. The joy with which his friend receives these glorious tidings, causes him to forget the wounds upon his head, which he has unluckily received by a too free and premature declaration of his principles. There is a fine contrast in the smile of innocence in the child at the woman's back, compared with the grim joy of a gentleman by it; while the hard countenance of its mother gives a delicacy to the grenadier's girl. Directly behind the drummer's *quondam* spouse, a soldier is reclining against a shed, near which is posted a quack-bill of Dr. Rock; and directly over him a wench at a wicket is archly taking a view, both of the soldier and of the march. Behind the drummer, under the sign of the Adam and Eve, are a group of figures, two of which are engaged in the fashionable art of bruising; their equal dexterity is shown by *sewed up peepers* on one side, and *a pate well sconced* on the other. And here the painter has shown his impartiality to the merit of our *noble youths* (who, their minds being inflamed with a love of glory, appear, not only encouragers of this truly laudable science, but many of them are also great proficients in the art itself), by introducing a youth of quality, whose face is expressive of those boisterous passions necessary to form a hero of this kind; and who, entering deep into the scene, endeavours to inspire the combatants with a noble contempt of bruises and broken bones. An old woman, moved by a foolish compassion, endeavours to force through the crowd, and part the fray, in which design she is stopped by a fellow who prefers fun and mischief to humanity. Above their heads appears *Jackey James*, a cobbler, a little man of meagre frame, but full of spirits, who enjoys the combat, and with fists clenched, in imagination deals blow for blow with the heroes. This figure is finely contrasted by a heavy, sluggish fellow just behind. The painter, with a stroke of humour peculiar to himself, has exhibited a figure shrinking under the load of a heavy box upon his back, who, preferring curiosity to ease, is a spectator, and waits, in this uneasy state, the issue of the combat. Upon a board next the sign, where roots, flowers, &c. were said to be sold, the painter has humourously altered the words *Tottenham Court Nursery*, alluding to a bruising booth then in that place, and the group of figures underneath.

"Passing through the turnpike, appears a carriage laden with the implements of war, as drums, halberds, tent-poles, and hoop-petticoats. Upon the carriage are two old women-campaigners, funking their pipes, and holding a conversation, as usual, in fire and smoke. The grotesque figures afford a fine contrast to a delicate woman upon the same carriage, who is suckling a child. This excellent figure evidently proves, that the painter is as capable of succeeding in the graceful style as in the humourous. A little boy lies at the feet of this figure; and the painter, to show him of martial breed, has placed a small trumpet in his mouth.

"The serious group of the principal figures in the centre is finely relieved by a scene of humour on the left. Here an officer has seized a milk wench, and is rudely kissing her. While the officer's ruffles suffer in this action, the girl pays her price, by an arch soldier, who, in her absence of attention to her pails, is filling his hat with milk, and, by his waggish eye, seems also to partake in the kissing scene. A chimney-sweeper's boy, with glee, puts in a request to the soldier, to supply him with a cap full when his own turn is served; while another soldier points out the fun to a fellow selling pies, who, with an inimitable face of simple joy, neglects the care of his goods, which the soldier dexterously removes with his other hand. In the figure of the pieman the pencil has exceeded all power of description. The old soldier, divested of one spatterdash, and near losing the other, is knocked down by all-potent gin: upon calling for *t'other cogue,* his waggish comrade, supporting him with one hand, endeavours to pour water into his mouth with the other, which the experienced old one rejects with disdain, puts up his hand to his wife, who bears the arms and gin-bottle, and who, well acquainted with his taste, is filling a quartern. Here the painter exhibits a sermon upon the excessive use of spirituous liquors, and the destructive consequences attending it; for the soldier is not only rendered incapable of his duty, but (what is shocking to behold) a child, with an emaciated countenance, extends its little arms with great earnestness, and wishes for that liquor of which it seems well acquainted with the taste. And here, not to dwell wholly upon the beauties of this painting, I must mention an absurdity discovered by a professed connoisseur in painting. 'Can there,' says he, 'be a greater absurdity than the introducing a couple of chickens so near a crowd? And not only so; but see!—their direction is to go to objects it is natural for them to shun. Is this knowledge of nature? Absurd to the last degree!' And here, with an air of triumph, ended our judicious critic. But how great was his surprise, when it was discovered to him, that the said chickens were in pursuit of the hen which had made her escape into the pocket of a soldier!

"Next the sign-post is an honest tar throwing up his hat, crying, 'God bless King George!' Before him is an image of drunken loyalty, who, with his shirt out of his breeches, and bayonet in his hand, vows destruction on the heads of the rebels. A fine figure of a speaking old woman, with a basket upon her head, will upon view tell you what she sells. A humane soldier, perceiving a fellow hard loaded with a barrel of gin upon his back, and stopped by the crowd, with a gimblet bores a hole in the head of the cask, and is kindly easing him of a part of his burthen. Near him is the figure of a fine gentleman in the army. As I suppose the painter designed him without character, I shall therefore only observe, that he is a very pretty fellow; and happily the contemplation of his own dear person guards him from the attempts of the wicked woman on his right hand. Upon the right of this *petit-maitre*, a licentious soldier is rude with a girl, who screams and wreaks her little vengeance upon his face, whilst his comrade is removing off some linen that hangs in his way.

"You will pardon the invention of a new term—I shall include the whole King's Head in the word *Cattery*, the principal figure of which is the famous *Mother Douglas*, who, with pious eyes cast up to heaven, prays for the army's success, and the safe return of many of her babes of grace. An officer offers a letter to one of this lady's children, who rejects it; possibly not liking the cause her spark is engaged in, or, what is more probable, his not having paid for her last favour. Above her, a charitable girl is throwing a shilling to a cripple, while another kindly administers a cordial to her companion, as a sure relief against reflection. The rest of the windows are full of the like cattle; and upon the house-top appear three cats, just emblems of the creatures below, but more harmless in their amorous encounter."

King George the Second was told that Hogarth had painted this picture, and wished to have the honour of dedicating to his Majesty the print engraved from it; and a proof-print was accordingly presented for his approbation. The king probably expected to see an allegorical representation of an army of heroes, devoting their lives to the service of their country and their sovereign; we may, therefore, readily conceive his disappointment on viewing their delineation. 'Does the fellow mean to laugh at my guards?' exclaimed the indignant monarch to a nobleman in waiting. 'The picture, please your Majesty, must be considered as a burlesque.' 'What! a painter burlesque a soldier? he deserves to be picketed for his insolence.' The print was returned to the artist, who, completely mortified at such a reception of what he properly considered to be his greatest work, immediately altered the inscription, inserting, instead of the King of England, "the King of Prusia (so spelt in the earliest impressions), an encourager of the Arts."

The following is another description of this Painting by Bonnell Thornton:—

"The scene is laid before the Adam and Eve, in Tottenham Court Road.

"A handsome young grenadier has been denominated the *principal figure,* but may, with more propriety, be called the principal figure of the principal group. His countenance exhibits a strong contest between affection and duty; for the manner in which his Irish *helpmate* clings to his arm, and, at the same time, with threatening aspect lifts up her right hand, grasping the *Remembrancer,* proves to a moral certainty, that to her he has made a matrimonial vow; while the tender, entreating distress of the poor girl at his right hand, seems to intimate, that though she possesses his heart, she can make no claim except to his gratitude and affection, both of which her present situation seems to demand.

"Her face forms a strong contrast to that of the fury, who is on the other side; for while one is marked with grief and tender regret, the other has all the savage ferocity of an unchained tiger: she is an accomplished masculine tramp, perfectly qualified to follow a regiment, and would be as ready to plunder those that are slaughtered, as to scold those who escape: being by no means of the class described by Doctor Johnson, when speaking of superfluous epithets, he says, 'they are like the valets and washerwomen that follow an army, who add to the number without increasing the force.' The papers, of which these two claimants are the vendors, determine their principles. The mild-tempered, soft-featured *gentlewoman,* with a cross upon a cloak, is evidently a hawker of the *Jacobites' Journal, Remembrancer,* and *London Evening Post,* papers remarkable for their inflammatory tendency, while a portrait of the gallant Duke of Cumberland, and the now popular ballad of *God save the King,* hang upon the basket of her rival.

"An old woman immediately behind, with a pipe in her mouth, and a child on her back, appears to have grown rather ancient in the service; but notwithstanding her load and her poverty, puffs away care, and carries a cheerful countenance.

"Near the child's head a meagre Frenchman is whispering an old fellow, who is called an *Independent;* but as in the original painting, part of a plaid appears under his great coat, the artist most probably intended him for an old highlander in disguise.

"A drummer, sick of the remonstrances of his wife and child, each of whom make a forcible seizure of his person, actuated by a spirit similar to that of our third Richard, beats a thundering tattoo upon his own warlike instrument; and aided by the *ear-piercing fife* at his right hand, drowns the noise of the *tell-tale woman*, who thus endeavours to check his ardour and impede his march.

"A war-worn soldier, contemplating a quack doctor's bill, and a woman peeping out of a pent-house above, end the group at the left corner.

"Under a sign of the Adam and Eve, a crowd are gathered round two combatants, who appear to be adepts in the noble science of boxing.

> "'Amid the circle now each champion stands,
> And poises high in air his iron hands;
> Hurling defiance; now they fiercely close—
> Their crackling jaws re-echo to the blows.'

"A man who, from his dress, seems to be of a rank superior to the crowd, inflamed with a love of glory, enters with great spirit into the business now going on, and tries to inspire the combatants with a noble contempt of bruises and broken bones. This is said to be a portrait of Lord Albemarle Bertie, who is again exhibited in the cock-pit. The scene being laid in the back-ground, the figures are diminutive, but every countenance is marked with interest; and no one more than a little fellow, of meagre frame, but undaunted spirit, who, with clenched fists and agitated face, deals blow for blow with the combatants. Somerville, in his 'Rural Games,' has well described the passions which agitate the audience, in a similar scene at a country wake:—

> " 'Each swain his wish, each trembling nymph conceals
> Her secret dread; while every panting breast
> Alternate fears and hopes depress or raise:
> Thus, long in dubious scale the contest hung,' &c.

"With a humour peculiar to himself, the painter has exhibited a figure shrinking under the weight of a heavy burden, who preferring the gratification of curiosity to rest, is a spectator, and in this uneasy state waits the issue of the combat.

"Upon the sign-board of the Adam and Eve is inserted, *Tottenham Court Nursery;* allusive to a booth for bruising in the place, as well as a nursery for plants, and the group of figures beneath.

"A carriage laden with *camp equipage*, consisting of drums, halberds, tent-poles, and hoop-petticoats, is passing through the turnpike-gate. Upon this two old female campaigners are puffing their pipes, and holding a conversation in fire and smoke. These grotesque personages are well contrasted by an elegant and singularly delicate figure upon the same carriage, suckling her child; which, it has been said, proves that the painter is as successful in pourtraying the graceful as the humourous. This very beautiful figure is, however, also a direct copy from Guido's Madonna. To shew that a little boy at her feet is of an heroic stock, the artist has represented him blowing a small trumpet. The serjeant on the ground beneath, seems exerting the authority with which his post vests him, in calling his men to order; he has a true roast beef countenance, and is haughty enough for a general. The foreground in the centre is occupied by a group of figures, which tell their own story in a manner that, perhaps, no other artist of any age could have equalled. While an officer is kissing a milk-maid, an arch soldier, taking advantage of her neglected pails, fills his hat with milk: this is observed by a little chimney-sweeper, who, with a grin upon his face, entreats that he may have a share in the plunder, and fills his cap. Another soldier, pointing out the jest to a fellow who is selling pies, the pastry-cook, gratified by the mischief, forgets the luscious cakes in the tray on his head, and the military *mercury* seems likely to *convey* them all to his own pocket. The faces of this group are, in a most singular degree, descriptive of their situations, and consonant to their mischievous employments.

"An old soldier, divested of one spatterdash, near losing the other, and felled to the ground by all-potent gin, is now calling for more; his uncivil comrade, supporting him with one hand, endeavours to pour water into his mouth with the other: this the veteran toper rejects with disdain, and lifts up a hand to his wife, who is the bearer of the arms and the bottle, and being well acquainted with his taste, fills *another quartern*.

"A child, with emaciated face, extends its little

arms, and wishes for a taste of that poisonous potion it is probably accustomed to swallow. And here, not to dwell wholly upon the *beauties* of this picture, I must mention an error discovered by a professed *connoisseur* in painting. ‘Can there,’ says this excellent judge, ‘be a greater absurdity than introducing a couple of chickens so near such a crowd: and not only so; but see!—their direction is to objects it is natural for them to shun. Is this knowledge of nature? Absurd to the last degree!’ And here, with an air of triumph, ended our judicious critic. How great was his surprise, when it was pointed out, that the said chickens were in pursuit of the hen, which appears to have a resting-place in a soldier's pocket.

“An honest tar, throwing up his hat, is crying *God save our noble King—God save the King:* immediately before him, an image of drunken loyalty vows *de—de—destruction* on the heads of the rebels.

“A humane soldier, perceiving a fellow heavily laden with a barrel of gin, and stopped by the crowd, bores a hole in the head of his cask, and kindly draws off a part of his burthen. Near him is a figure of what may, in the army, be called a fine fellow. As I suppose the painter designed him without character, I shall only observe, that he is a very pretty gentleman; and happily, the contemplation of his own dear person guards him from the attempts of the wicked woman on his right hand.

“The invention of a new term must be pardoned; I shall include the whole *King's Head* in the word *cattery.* The principal figure is a noted fat Covent Garden lady, who, with pious eyes cast up into heaven, prays for the army's success, and the safe return of many of her babes of grace. An officer, having placed a letter on the end of his pike, presents it to one of the beauties in the first floor; but the fair *enamorata,* evidently disgusted at the recollection of some part of his former conduct, flutters her fan, and rejects it with disdain. Above her, a charitable girl, of an inferior order, is throwing a piece of coin to a cripple, while another kindly administers *a glass of comfort* to her companion, as a sure relief against reflection. The rest of the windows are crowded with similar characters; and upon the house-top, is a *cat coterie,* a fair emblem of the company in the apartments beneath.

"That so admirable a representation of the manners of *England* should be dedicated to the King of Prussia, is one of those odd circumstances which must surprise a man who is not acquainted with the history of the plate. Before publication, it was inscribed to George the Second, and the picture taken to St. James's, in the hope of *royal* approbation. George the Second was *an honest man, and a soldier,* but not a judge of either a work of humour or a work of art. The corporal or serjeant he considered as employed in a way which dignified their nature, and gave them a title to the name and rank of gentlemen. The painter or engraver, however exquisite their skill, or however elevated their conceptions, were, on the king's scale, mere mechanics.

"When told that Hogarth had painted a picture of the guards on their march to *Finchley*, and meant to dedicate a print engraved from it to the King of Great Britain, his Majesty probably expected to see an allegorical representation of an army of heroes, devoting their lives to the service of their country, and their sovereign habited like *the mailed Mars*, seated upon a cloud, where he might,

'—— with a commanding voice,
Cry havock, and let slip the dogs of war.'

"If such was his expectation, we may readily conceive his disappointment on viewing this delineation. His first question was addressed to a nobleman in waiting—'Pray, who is this Hogarth?' 'A painter, my liege.' 'I hate *bainting* and *boetry* too! Neither the one nor the other ever did any good! Does the fellow mean to laugh at my guards?' 'The picture, an' please your Majesty, must undoubtedly be considered as a burlesque.' 'What! a *bainter* burlesque a soldier? He deserves to be picketed for his insolence! Take his trumpery out of my sight.'

"The print was returned to the artist, who, completely mortified at such a reception of what he very properly considered as his first work, immediately altered the inscription, inserting, instead of the King of England, the *King of Prusia, an encourager of the arts and sciences!*"

A LARGE SEA-PIECE,

Representing Ships employed in the British Navy, in various positions.

By BROOKING.

This painter had been in some department in the dock-yard at Deptford, but practised as a ship-painter, in which he excelled all his countrymen, nor have any since Vandervelde equalled his productions in that department of painting; but his merit being scarcely known before his death, prevented him from acquiring the honour and profit which, by his abilities, he had a just right to expect. He died of a consumption, at his lodging in Castle Street, Leicester Square, in the spring of the year 1759, under forty years of age.

The following anecdote is given upon the authority of the late Mr. D. Sertes, to whom he was well known:—

"Many of the artists of that time worked for the shops, and Brooking, like the rest, painted much for a person who lived in Castle Street, Leicester Square, who coloured prints, and dealt in pictures, which he exposed at his shop-window. A gentleman,* who sometimes passed the shop, being struck with the merits of some sea-pieces, which were by the hand of this artist, desired to know his name; but his enquiries were not answered agreeably to his wishes:

* Mr. Taylor White, then Treasurer of the Foundling Hospital.

he was only told, that if he pleased, they could procure any that he might require from the same painter. Brooking was accustomed to write his name upon his pictures, which mark was as constantly obliterated by the shop-keeper before he placed them in his window: it however happened that the artist carried home a piece, on which his name was inscribed, while the master was not at home, and the wife, who received it, placed it in the window without effacing the signature. Luckily, the gentleman passed by before this picture was removed, and discovered the name of the painter whose works he so justly admired. He immediately advertised for the artist to meet him at a certain wholesale linen-draper's in the city. To this invitation Brooking at first paid no regard; but seeing it repeated, with assurances of benefit to the person to whom it was addressed, he prudently attended, and had an interview with the gentleman, who, from that time, became his friend and patron. Unfortunately, the artist did not live long enough to gratify the wishes of his benefactor, or to receive any very great benefit from his patronage."

A LANDSCAPE.

By GEORGE LAMBERT.

Lambert was, for many years, principal scene painter to the theatre at Covent Garden. Being a person of great respectability in character and profession, he was often visited, while at work in the theatre, by persons of the first consideration, both in rank and talents. As it frequently happened that he was too much hurried to leave his engagements for his regular dinner, he contented himself with a beef steak, broiled upon the fire in the painting-room. In this hasty meal he was sometimes joined by his visitors, who were pleased to participate in the humble repast of the artist. The flavour of the dish, and the conviviality of the accidental meeting, inspired the party with a resolution to establish a club, which was accordingly done, under the title of "The Beef Steak Club;" and the party assembled in the painting-room. The members were afterwards accommodated with a room in the play-house, where the meetings were held for many years; but after the theatre was last rebuilt, the place of assembly was changed to the Shakspeare Tavern.

Another circumstance in this gentleman's life is better worth recording, as being more intimately acquainted with the arts. When the artists had formed themselves into a regular society, and obtained a charter of incorporation, Lambert was nominated the president, being the first person who was appointed to that honourable station; but this distinction was of very short duration, for he did not survive the signature of the charter above four days. He died 30th January, 1765.

ELIJAH RAISING THE SON OF THE WIDOW OF ZAREPHATH.

"*And he stretched himself upon the child three times, and cried unto the Lord, and said, O Lord my God, I pray thee let this child's soul come into him again.*

And the Lord heard the voice of Elijah, and the soul of the child came into him again, and he revived."

BY LANFRANCO.

This picture was presented by Mr. Langford, a well-known fashionable auctioneer and a zealous friend of the charity whose name appears with those of the artists dining at the Hospital in 1757.

PORTRAIT OF HANDEL.

BY SIR GODFREY KNELLER.

Sir Godfrey Kneller was born at Lubec about the year 1648. He was at first designed for a military life, and was sent to Leyden, where he applied himself to mathematics and fortification, but the predominance of nature determining him to painting, his father acquiesced, and sent him to Amsterdam, where he studied under Bol, and had some instruction from Rembrandt. After this he came to England, and obtained great popularity in his profession at Court and otherwise.

He painted Dryden in his own hair, in plain drapery, holding a laurel, and made him a present of the work. The poet repaid this by an epistle containing encomiums such as few painters deserve:—

> "Such are thy pictures, Kneller! such thy skill,
> That nature seems obedient to thy will;
> Comes out and meets thy pencil in the draught,
> Lives there, and wants but words to speak the thought."

To the incense of Dryden was added that of Pope, Addison, Prior, Tickell, and Steele. No wonder the artist was vain. But the vanity of Kneller was redeemed by his *naïveté*, and rendered pleasant by his wit. "Dost thou think, man," said he to his tailor, who proposed his son for a pupil, "dost thou think, man, I can make thy son a painter? No! God Almighty only makes painters." His wit, however, was that of one who had caught the spirit of Charles the Second's wicked court. He once overheard a low fellow cursing himself. "God damn you, indeed!" exclaimed the artist, in wonder; "God may damn the Duke of Marlborough, and perhaps Sir Godfrey Kneller; but do you think He will take the trouble of damning such a scoundrel as you?" The servants of his neighbour, Dr. Ratcliffe, abused the liberty of a private entrance to the painter's garden, and plucked his flowers. Kneller sent word, that he must shut the door up. "Tell him," the Doctor peevishly replied, "that he may do anything with it but paint it." "Never mind what he says," retorted Sir Godfrey, "I can take anything from him—but physic."

Kneller was one day conversing about his art,

when he gave the following neat reason for preferring portraiture:—"Painters of history," said he, "make the dead live, and do not begin to live themselves till they are dead. I paint the living, and they make me live!" In a conversation concerning the legitimacy of the unfortunate son of James the Second, some doubts having been expressed by an Oxford Doctor, he exclaimed with much warmth, "His father and mother have sat to me about thirty-six times a-piece, and I know every line and bit of their faces. Mein Gott! I could paint King James's *now* by memory. I say the child is so like both, that there is not a feature in his face but what belongs either to father or to mother; this I am sure of, and cannot be mistaken: nay, the nails of his fingers are his mother's, the queen that was. Doctor, you may be out in your letters, but I cannot be out in my lines."

PORTRAIT IN CRAYONS OF TAYLOR WHITE, Esq.,

(Treasurer of the Hospital from 1746 *to* 1771*)*

By FRANCIS COTES, R.A.

The father of Cotes was an apothecary of great respectability, residing in Cork Street, Burlington Gardens, and his son was the pupil of Mr. Knapton, but, in the sequel, much excelled his master. He was particularly eminent for his portraits in crayons, in which branch of the art he surpassed all his predecessors, though, it must be confessed he owed something of his excellence to the study of the portraits of Rosalba. He also painted with considerable ability in oil colours; and, if Hogarth's opinion could be considered as oracular, excelled Reynolds as a portrait-painter. But though his portraits in oil were by no means so masterly as those of his rival, yet they were very pleasing and well finished, coloured with great spirit, and, by the aid of Mr. Tom's draperies, were deservedly ranked with the best portraits of the time.

Cotes was in very excellent practice as a painter in oil; but his chief excellence, as before observed, was in crayons, which were greatly improved under his hands, both in their preparation and application. Walpole has given a list of some of his principal portraits in crayons, to which may be added, the whole-length of Queen Charlotte with the Princess Royal in her lap, which he painted in oil, about the year 1767. He was very early in life afflicted with the stone, and, before he attained the age of forty-five, he fell a victim to that disease. He died at his house in Cavendish Square, July 20th, 1770, and was buried at Richmond, in Surrey.

PORTRAIT IN CRAYONS OF GEORGE WHATLEY, Esq.,

(Treasurer of the Hospital from 1779 to 1791)

By A PERSON UNKNOWN.

PORTRAIT OF CHARLES POTT, Esq.

The present Treasurer, whom God preserve!

This Portrait was painted by the late eminent artist,

THOMAS PHILLIPS, Esq., R.A.

Its origin will be better explained by the following extract from the Minutes of the Court of Governors of the 12th May, 1841.

"A Governor in his place, stated to the Court, that several Members of the Corporation, being sensible of the great services rendered to the Charity by the Treasurer, Charles Pott, Esq., were anxious to testify their individual approbation of the able and zealous manner in which he has performed the duties of his office, and had therefore entered upon a subscription in the hope that he would oblige them by sitting to an eminent artist for his portrait, with the view of its being placed in some suitable situation within the walls of the Hospital.

"The Chairman having communicated this desire to the Treasurer, obtained his acquiescence."

THE VESTIBULE.

THE OFFERING OF THE WISE MEN.

"*And when they were come into the house, they saw the young child, with Mary, his mother, and fell down and worshipped him, and when they had opened their treasures, they presented unto him gifts; gold, and frankincense, and myrrh.*"

By ANDREW CASALI,

Commonly called Chevalier, an Italian, said to have been a native of Civita Vecchia. At what time he came to England is not ascertained, but he was in London before the year 1748, for he was employed to paint the transparencies which formed a part of the decorations of the fireworks exhibited in the Green Park, St. James's, on the celebration of the peace of Aix-la-Chapelle, which pictures were for many years to be seen in the Ordnance Office at the Tower. He was much employed by the elder Mr. Beckford, at Fonthill, where he painted some ceilings. He was one of the first candidates for the premium offered by the Society of Arts, Manufactures, and Commerce, for the best historical picture, the subject to be taken from the English history; and in the year 1760, he obtained the second premium, fifty guineas; in 1761 and again in 1762, he obtained the first premium, one hundred guineas; and in 1766, for an historical picture in *chiaro scuro*, the first premium, fifty guineas. At the time the Foundling Hospital was completed, he painted the above picture for the altar of the Chapel, which he presented to the Charity. This picture remained several years in its primitive situation, but was removed to make way for the picture of West, which now occupies the place.

Of the hand of Casali, there are also two figures of St. Peter and St. Paul, in *chiaro scuro*, at the altar of St. Margaret's Church, Westminster. These figures were painted about the year 1758. This artist's productions are said to be carefully painted, clean in their execution, showy, but tawdry in the colouring.

ACTION OFF THE COAST OF FRANCE,

May 13th, 1779.

By LUNY.

The particulars of this Picture are as follows, viz.

"*Sir James Wallace, Commander of H. M. Ship Experiment, with the Pallas, Unicorn, Fortunæ, and Cabot, Brigs, attacking the Danæ, Valeur, Recluce, three French Frigates, and a Cutter, in Concale Bay. The Danæ he brought off. The other three being aground, he burnt, amidst a smart fire from a battery of six twelve-pounders, and several cannon from the shore. The battery he silenced in half an hour.*"

PORTRAIT OF LORD CHIEF JUSTICE WILMOT,

By DANCE.

The members of the family to which this eminent judge belonged were, from an early period, liberal supporters of the Hospital, and it is to a collateral branch, namely, — The Right Honourable Lord Saye and Sele, that the Governors are indebted for this picture.

It is worthy of remark that the Foundling Hospital has been supported, from time to time, by some of the most distinguished judges who have adorned the Bench.

BUST OF HANDEL,

By LOUIS FRANCIS ROUBILIAC.

Roubiliac, who was born at Lyons, in France, became a formidable rival to Rysbrack. He had little business, till Sir Edward Walpole* recommended him for the execution of all the busts at Trinity College, Dublin; and, by the same patron's interest, he was employed on the monument of the Duke of Argyle, in Westminster Abbey. His statue of Handel, in the gardens at Vauxhall, fixed Roubiliac's fame. Two of his principal works are the monuments of the late Duke and Duchess of Montagu, in Northamptonshire. His statue of George the First, in the Senate House at Cambridge, is said to be well executed; and so is that of their then Chancellor, Charles, Duke of Somerset. His statue of Sir Isaac Newton, in the chapel of Trinity College, is considered the best of the three. This able artist had a turn to poetry, and

---

* Roubiliac is said to have gained the Patronage of Sir Edward Walpole in this singular manner. Very soon after he arrived in England, and was then working as journeyman to Carter, a maker of monuments, having spent an evening at Vauxhall, on his return he picked up a pocket-book, which he found to enclose several Bank Notes of value. He immediately advertised the circumstance—and a gentleman of fashion, Sir Edwarl Walpole, claimed the pocket-book. Justly appreciating and remunerating the integrity of the poor young man, and the specimens of his skill and talent which he exhibited, he promised to patronize him through life, and he faithfully performed this promise.

wrote satires in French verse. He died January 11th, 1762, and was buried in the parish of St. Martin's, where he lived.

The above bust was taken by the artist, from sittings to him by Handel, and is the original work from which the celebrated statue in Vauxhall Gardens and that in Westminster Abbey were made. At the sale of Mr. Barrett, the proprietor of Vauxhall Gardens, the bust was purchased by Mr. Bartleman, and was, for many years, esteemed by him as his greatest treasure. Upon his death, it passed, by sale, into the hands of the trade; and lastly, upon the recommendation of Mr. William Behnes, sculptor, was purchased and presented to the Hospital by Sir Frederick Pollock, one of the Vice-Presidents, now Lord Chief Baron of the Exchequer.

There is also in the Vestibule a model of the late Sir William Curtis, Bart. by Sievier, after a portrait by Sir Thomas Lawrence. This is considered an excellent likeness of the worthy baronet, whose son, the present Sir William Curtis, is one of the Vice-Presidents of the Hospital, and has been for more than thirty years its zealous friend and able supporter.

Besides this model, there are two busts, namely, one (by Behnes) of the late Henry Earle, Esq., the eminent Surgeon, who gratuitously gave his professional services to the Children of the Hospital for many years.

The other of the present Morning Preacher, by S. J. B. Haydon.

DINING HALLS.

PORTRAIT OF GEORGE THE SECOND,

(First Patron of the Hospital)

BY SHACKLETON.

John Shackleton was principal painter to the Crown in the latter end of the reign of George II. and until his death, which happened March 16th, 1767.

PORTRAIT OF THE EARL OF DARTMOUTH,

(A Vice-President of the Hospital)

BY SIR JOSHUA REYNOLDS.

An account of Sir Joshua Reynolds might appear superfluous here, but he was so zealous a friend of the Charity, and passed so much of his time within its walls, that this compilation would be incomplete without some notice of this most eminent and good man.* Sir Joshua was born at Plympton, in Devonshire, July 16th, 1723. His father, the Rev. Samuel Reynolds, was master of the free grammar school of that town. The son received his school education from his father. When very young he discovered a

* So late as 1782, we still find him taking an interest in the Hospital. "I beg" (he says, in a letter to the secretary) " my respectful compliments may be presented to the governors. I consider the nomination of myself to be one of the stewards as a great honour conferred on me, and will certainly attend at the Hospital on the anniversary in May next."

strong inclination to painting, which was confirmed by his reading Richardson's Treatise on that art. This natural propensity was indulged and strengthened at intervals, by copies which he made after the various prints he could then procure; among which were the frontispieces to Plutarch's Lives, and also Jacob Catts' Emblems. When he was of age to assume a profession, he was placed with Mr. Hudson, who was at that time the most fashionable portrait-painter. This situation was wisely chosen by the father, as being congenial to the natural inclinations of the son. When he quitted Hudson, he returned to Devonshire, where he pursued the practice of portrait-painting. He began his career at a very low price, by which he gained not only employment but improvement, and he improved his taste by visiting the Continent more than once.

At his first establishment he resided in St. Martin's Lane, but soon removed to a large mansion on the north-side of Great Newport Street, where he dwelt a few years. In 1761, he removed to the west-side of Leicester Square, where he bought a good house, to which he added a very convenient painting-room, and an elegant gallery for the display of his pictures. In 1765, he exhibited a whole-length of Lady Sarah Bunbury, who in the picture is represented as sacrificing to the Graces. Thus he introduced into his portraits a style of gallant compliment which proved that, as a painter, he well knew how to ensure the approbation of the distinguished fair. At this time he had attained the summit of his reputation as an artist, which he maintained till the close of his life, although Cotes, and afterwards Ramsay, shared in no small degree the fashion of the day.

Though he subscribed his name on the roll of the Charter of the Society of Artists, at their incorporation, and was appointed one of the directors, yet he took little or no part in the business of that Institution. The conduct of the refractory members of the Chartered Society having given rise to the Royal Academy, Reynolds was chosen President. Upon this occasion he received the honour of knighthood, and on the 2nd January, 1769, took his seat for the first time as President, when he delivered a discourse to the Royal Academicians, replete with candour, sound sense, and the most suitable advice to those who had the conduct of the schools then newly established. This practice he continued, as often as the gold medals were bestowed upon those students of the Academy who had produced the best historical picture. Some years before, he had obtained the intimacy and friendship of many of the first literary characters of the age, and had shewn himself capable of employing his pen as an able critic in his profession, for in the year 1759, he wrote three letters, which were inserted in the *Idler*, a periodical paper, supported by his intimate friend Dr. Samuel Johnson. Sir Joshua died in the year 1792, in the sixty-ninth year of his age.

PORTRAIT OF THE EARL OF MACCLESFIELD,

(A Vice-President)

By WILSON.

Of whom an account has already been given.

PORTRAIT OF Dr. MEAD,

(A very active Governor)

By ALLAN RAMSAY.

Mr. Ramsay was the son of Allan Ramsay, author of the pastoral drama, called, "The Gentle Shepherd,"—he was born in Edinburgh.

As an artist, he is said to have been rather self-taught, but went early in life to Italy, where he reived some instructions from *Solimene*, and also from *Imperiale*, two artists of much celebrity in that country. After his return, he practised for some time in Edinburgh, but chiefly in London, and acquired a considerable degree of reputation in his profession.

By the interest of Lord Bute, he was introduced to George III. when Prince of Wales, whose portrait he painted, both at whole-length and also in profile. Beside these, there are several mezzotinto prints, after pictures which he painted, of some of the principal personages among his countrymen. Though he did not acquire the highest degree of rank in his profession, yet he practised with considerable success for many years, and at the death of Mr. Shackleton, which was in March, 1767, he was appointed principal painter to the Crown, a situation which he retained till his death, though he retired from practise about eight years after his appointment.

Although Ramsay, as a painter, did not acquire that vigour of execution and brilliancy of colouring which distinguished the works of Sir Joshua Reynolds, yet his portraits possess a calm representation of nature, that much exceeds the mannered affectation of squareness which prevailed among his cotemporary artists; and it may be justly allowed, that he was among the first of those who contributed to improve the degenerated style of portrait-painting. That he possessed a considerable degree of public notice, may be presumed from the following observation of Walpole, who says, that "Reynolds and Ramsay have wanted subjects, not genius;" but the truth is, that if the latter possessed equal genius with the former, he still wanted that affection to his art, which, added to his natural taste, were the constant stimuli to Sir Joshua's exertions, and the cause of his great superiority above his brother artists.

Dr. Mead was an early and a very zealous Governor of the Hospital. He was the most eminent physician of his time, and was born at Stepney, 11th August, 1673. In 1702 he published a work called

" Mechanical Account of Poisons," and subsequently other valuable treatises. He was one of the members of the Royal Society when Sir Isaac Newton was the president, and was physician to St. Thomas's Hospital. He died at his house in Great Ormond Street, in 1754.

PORTRAITS OF THEODORE JACOBSEN, Esq.,

(The Architect of the Hospital)

AND JOHN MILNER, Esq.,

(A Governor)

By THOMAS HUDSON.

Hudson, who was the pupil and son-in-law of Richardson, enjoyed for many years the chief business of portrait-painting in the capital, after the favourite artists, his master and Jervas, were gone off the stage, though Vanloo first, and Liotard afterwards, for a few years, diverted the torrent of fashion from the established profession. Still the country gentlemen were faithful to their compatriot, and were content with his honest similitudes, and with the fair tied wigs, blue velvet coats, and white satin waistcoats, which he bestowed liberally on his customers. The better taste introducing Sir Joshua Reynolds (who was his pupil for two years), put an end to Hudson's reign, who had the good sense to resign the throne soon after finishing his capital

B. Nibot pinx.t J. W. Cook, sculp.t

CAPTAIN THOMAS CORAM.

work—the Family Piece of Charles, Duke of Marlborough.

He retired to a small villa he had built at Twickenham, on a most beautiful part of the river, and where he furnished the best rooms with a well-chosen collection of cabinet pictures and drawings by great masters, having purchased many of the latter from his father-in-law's capital collection. Towards the end of his life, he was married to his second wife, Mrs. Fiennes, a gentlewoman with a good fortune, to whom he bequeathed his villa, and died January 26th, 1779, aged seventy-eight.

PORTRAIT OF CAPTAIN CORAM,

(The Founder)

BY HOGARTH.

Captain Coram was born at Lyme Regis, in Dorsetshire, in the year 1668. He was a descendant of the Corhams, of Devonshire; and Kinterbury, in that county, was, for several generations, the property and residence of the family.* Of his baptism, there does not appear to be any record at Lyme Regis; and all that can be found in the registers relating to the family is the following: —

"William, son of John Coram, Captain, was baptized at Lyme, April 29th, 1671."†

* Vide Risdon's Chorographical Description of the County of Devon.

† For this information the writer is indebted to Dr. Hodges, the present Vicar of Lyme Regis.

There seems to be no doubt, therefore, that this "William" was a younger brother of "Thomas," the subject of this memoir, and consequently, that the latter, in devoting himself to the sea service, followed the occupation of his father. At Lyme Regis, which is a sea-port, there was carried on, at the period in question, a considerable coasting and Newfoundland trade; and hence we may venture to account for the first direction of his course in maritime concerns.

Of his early years there is no biographical notice extant; but it appears probable, that the ardent temperament which he exhibited through life, was too strong for the restraints of home and domestic ties, and that this, and his love of enterprise, caused him to be, even at the outset of his career, an independent member of his father's family.*

About the year 1694, (he being then twenty-six years old), we find him at Taunton,† Massachusetts,

---

* Mrs. Thomasine Shepheard, now residing at Plymouth, who is grand-niece of the Founder of the Hospital, has in her possession several relics, including a silver cup, which he presented, in 1727, to his god-son, "Thomas Corham."

† This information is furnished by the Rev. N. T. Bent, of Massachusetts, conveyed by the following letter:—

"Taunton, Mass., Oct. 14, 1844.

"Dear Sir,

"When my friend and parishioner, Mr. W. A. Crocker, was in London, in 1841, you were kind enough to put in his hands several pamphlets, containing references to that excellent man, Thomas Coram. I have the pleasure now to send you a few copies of a discourse, historical of St. Thomas's Church, in this town. One chief object in its publication was, to rescue from forgetfulness the name and deeds of that eminent philanthropist, little known in this country, I presume, but richly deserving commemoration.

"We have become warmly attached to his memory; and, as I have inti-

in the United States, exercising the humble trade of a shipwright. To this new country he had, doubtless, gone in the spirit of adventure; and here he gave the first instance on record of that public devotedness for which he was so remarkable. Whilst in this comparative wilderness, he perceived, with regret, the uncivilized condition of the inhabitants,

---

mated in a note to the discourse, wish to place here some enduring memorial of the man. We have supposed that the object might enlist the sympathies of those, with you, who honour his name. Our plan is to erect a chapel, which shall be named for him, and bear on its walls a tablet to his memory—the same to be in connection with St. Thomas's Church, and under the control of its vestry. For such a chapel there is need amongst us, and it would essentially promote, we believe, the cause of that church which Captain Coram loved, and which, it is becoming more and more apparent, is the chief hope of our country. The members of St. Thomas's are zealous churchmen, and have already made the most generous efforts for the cause of the church in this town. But so few amongst them are blessed with the means of contributing, that it would be impossible for us to complete our present design within ourselves.

"Under these circumstances, rather than abandon an object upon which we have quite set our hearts, we venture to appeal to yourself; and should the matter strike you favourably, through you to others. I can but hope you will find it possible to promote this object. Could we secure, through yourself, a subscription of £200 or £300, we could then worthily carry out our plan.

"May I ask you to consider the matter, and if you judge best, to present a subscription for the object to such as you think might favour it. If, in this request, I have presumed too much upon your interest in the subject, my own must be the apology.

"Our desire is, to complete a subscription for the chapel at once. May I hope to hear from you, in reply to this, at an early day. Should further information be desired, it will be cheerfully given.

"Commending the matter to the kind regards of yourself and friends,

"I am, my dear Sir,

"Very truly, your obedient Servant,

"N. T. Bent."

"J. Brownlow, Esq.,
Foundling Hospital, London."

by reason of the absence of systematic religion, as exercised by the Church of England, of which he was a member. By a deed, therefore, dated 8th December, 1703, he conveyed to the governor and other authorities of Taunton, fifty-nine acres of land. The condition of the gift was this,—that whenever, in the progress of civilization and the increase of population, the people of the place should desire the Church of England to be established there, that then, on their application to the vestrymen, or their successors in office, the land, or a suitable part of it, was to be granted for that purpose, or for a school-house, as they might desire. This gift, the deed alleges, was made "in consideration of the love and respect which the donor had and did bear unto the said church, as also for divers other good causes and considerations him especially at that present moving." In this deed he is described as "of Boston, in New England, sometimes residing in Taunton, in the County of Bristol, Shipwright." At a subsequent period of his life he presented to the parish of Taunton a valuable library, part of which remains to this day. Some of the books appear to have been solicited by Coram from others. Thus, in the copy of Common Prayer now preserved in the church, the entry in the title page is as follows:—"This Book of Common Prayer is given by the Right Honourable Arthur Onslow, Speaker of the Honourable House of Commons of Great Britain, one of His Majesty's Most Honourable Privy Council, and Treasurer of His Majesty's Navy, &c., to *Thomas Coram*, of London, *Gentleman,* for the use of a Church lately built at Taunton, in New England." Coram appears to have obtained the warm friendship of Mr. Speaker Onslow, of the evidence of which this is not the only instance.

From Taunton Captain Coram removed to Boston, about the close of the seventeenth century, and engaged in commerce. He became a ship-master, and acquired some property in following the seas, especially in the then newly-discovered fisheries. By his intercourse with the colonies, at their different ports, he became well acquainted with their wants, and deeply concerned for their welfare; and though in a comparatively humble station, originated many noble plans for their benefit.

In 1704 he was very instrumental in planning and procuring an Act of Parliament, for encouraging the making of Tar in the Northern Colonies of British America, by a bounty to be paid on the importation thereof, whereby not only a livelihood was afforded to thousands of families employed in that branch of trade in North America, but above a million sterling was saved to the nation, which was heretofore obliged to buy all its Tar from Sweden, at a most exorbitant price, besides being imported in Swedish vessels.

In the year 1719, he was on board the ship, "Sea Flower" on her passage to Hamburgh, when she was stranded off Cuxhaven and plundered by the inhabitants of the district of her cargo. Coram, in endeavouring to preserve the property on board, was grossly illused by the pirates, who managed to overpower him and the rest of the authorities. In the affidavit relating to this outrage, he is described as "of London, Mariner and Shipwright," and the affidavit further sets forth, "That he (Coram) having usually sold to his Majesty in the year past and at other times, quantities of naval stores from America, for the supply of his Majesty's navy, did about February last, design to visit his Majesty's German Dominions to see what supplies of timber and other naval stores could be had from thence, fit for the navy royal." By this incident in the life of Coram, we learn the nature of his transactions at this period, but it would seem that soon afterwards, having accumulated as much wealth as suited his moderate views, he retired from the sea service and devoted himself for the remainder of his life to projects having for their object the public good. It was soon after this, that he turned his attention to the destitute state of the infant poor of the metropolis, and engaged in his laudable design of establishing an Hospital for Foundlings.

Captain Coram was not a mere theorist. All his schemes were of a practical nature. He first made himself thoroughly master of his subject, and then set about convincing those whose assistance he deemed necessary for their accomplishment. The difficulty he had to encounter was the want of that energy of character in others, which was so remarkable in himself. This retarded the progress of many of the projects he had set on foot for the benefit of mankind. The good, however, that he effected is sufficiently substantial to hand his name down to the latest posterity as the lover of his country and of her people. The celebrated Horace Walpole said of him that he was "the honestest, the most disinterested, and the most knowing person about the plantations" he ever talked with. The Colonial concerns of the country certainly had his special care.

It was at the solicitation of Captain Coram, that an Act of Parliament was obtained for taking off the prohibition on importing deal boards and fir timber from the Netherlands and Germany, on account of the King of Denmark having enhanced the prices of those commodities, by which means they immediately fell twenty per cent.

In the year 1732 he was appointed one of the trustees, by a charter from George II. for the settlement of Georgia, in the colonization of which province he took a deep interest.

His next project related to Nova Scotia, and about the year 1735 he addressed the following Memorial to George II.

"*To the King's Most Excellent Majesty in Council.*

"The Memorial of Thomas Coram, Gentleman, most humbly showeth,—

"That your memorialist having, through long experience in naval affairs, and by residing many years in your Majesty's plantations in America, observed, with attention, several matters and things which he conceives might be greatly improved, for the honour and service of the Crown, and the increase of the trade, navigation, and wealth of this kingdom; he, therefore, most humbly begs leave to represent to your Majesty,—

"That the coasts of your Majesty's province of *Nova Scotia* afford the best cod-fishing of any in the known parts of the world, and the land is well adapted for raising hemp, and other naval stores, for the better supplying this kingdom with the same: but the discouragements have hitherto been such as have deterred people from settling there, whereby the said province, for want of good inhabitants, is not so beneficial to this kingdom, nor so well secured to the Crown as it might be; because it cannot be presumed the French inhabitants, who remain there by virtue of the treaty, whereby *Nova Scotia* was surrendered to Great Britain, anno, 1710, being all papist, would be faithful to your Majesty's interest, in case of a war between Great Britain and France.

"Your memorialist, therefore, most humbly conceives, that it would be highly conducive to the interests of this kingdom, to settle, without loss of time, a competent number of industrious protestant families in the said province, which is the northern frontier of your Majesty's dominions in America, under a civil government to be established by your Majesty, conformable in all its branches, as near as may be to the constitution of England, which seems the most probable, if not the only means of people-ing this province, which experience shows could not be effected under the military government that hath been exercised there upward of twenty-four years past, and of giving effectual encouragement to the cod fishery, that valuable branch of the British commerce, which hath declined very much of late years, in proportion as the French have advanced therein.

"Your memoralist further begs leave to observe that the French are masters of the best salt in the world for curing fish, whereas the English are obliged to have what salt they use from foreign dominions, which make it highly necessary to secure a perpetual supply of salt in your Majesty's dominions in America, that we may not depend on a precarious supply of that commodity from the dominions of other princes. And your memoralist humbly conceives that the Island of Exuma, which is one of the Bahamas, would afford sufficient quantities of salt for all your Majesty's subjects in North America, provided Cat Island, another of the Bahamas, lying to windward of Exuma, was well settled and put in such a posture as to be able to cover Exuma and protect the salt rakers from the depredations of the Spaniards of Baracoa (the settling of Cat Island would be otherwise vastly advantageous to the Crown), and provided the unreasonable demand of the tenth of all salt raked there be abolished, for want of which encouragements, the salt ponds of Exuma have hitherto been useless to the public.

"To these purposes your memoralist humbly lays

the annexed petition at your Majesty's feet, and begs leave to add that there are several honourable and worthy persons ready to accept and act in the trust therein described, if your Majesty shall be pleased to grant your Royal Letters Patent for that purpose.

"Wherefore he most humbly prays your Majesty to order that this memorial, together with the petition hereunto annexed, and whatever your memorialist shall have occasion further to offer, concerning the same, may be taken into consideration, and that your Majesty will be graciously pleased to do therein as your Majesty in your great wisdom and goodness shall seem proper.

"And he will ever pray, &c., &c.

"THOMAS CORAM."

Accompanying this memorial, was a petition from more than one hundred "labouring handicraftsmen, whose respective trades and callings were overstocked by great numbers of artizans and workmen who resort from all parts of the metropolis, whereby the petitioners were unable to procure sufficient to maintain themselves and families." They further set forth "that to avoid extreme want, and escape the temptations which always attend poverty, they were desirous of being settled securely in some of the plantations of America." The petitioners then state the advantages of the uncultivated tracts of land in the province of Nova Scotia, and pray that they may have the grant of a free passage thither, and when there be protected, their persons and properties by a civil government as near as may be to the constitution of England.

Captain Coram's memorial was referred to the Lords Commissioners for Trade and Plantations, before whom he appeared on several occasions between the years 1735 and 1737, and both verbally and in writing submitted the most satisfactory and elaborate evidence of the propriety and expediency of his proposal, and the laws by which the colony should be maintained and governed, so as to draw the following approval from the Lords Commissioners, addressed to the Privy Council, dated 22nd April, 1737.

"The settlement of Nova Scotia with English inhabitants is of very great consequence to his Majesty's interest in America, and to the interest of this kingdom, from its situation with regard to the French, and from the fishery now carried on at Conso, and the several branches of naval stores that province is capable of producing, when once it shall be settled, as we have several times represented to his Majesty and to your lordships, particularly in our report of the 7th June, 1727; and therefore, we think it very much for his Majesty's service, to give all possible encouragement to any undertaking for this purpose, especially when attended with so great an appearance and probability of success as that of Mr. Coram's, now under our consideration."

Although the object which Captain Coram had in this matter was postponed for several years, owing to political changes and hindrances, yet, before he died, he had the satisfaction of seeing the full developement of his plans, in regard to this now valuable colony.

What further relates to this great and good man, and of the different measures which were the objects of his laborious and useful life, cannot be communicated more appropriately than in the language of Dr. Brocklesby, his most intimate friend, who, soon after the death of Coram, thus delineated his character.

"The tribute of praise is due to every virtue—due in proportion to the excellence and extent of that virtue to which it is paid; and consequently, public spirit, which is of all virtues the most conducive to the good of society, deserves as high returns of public gratitude and respect as can possibly be given. This is the rather incumbent on every community where conspicuous instances of this kind appear, because it is indeed the only reward adequate to their merit, and the best method of propagating the example; for what can so properly, or so potently excite public spirit, as the sense of its begetting public love? The most illustrious of all good qualities ought certainly to be honoured with the noblest testimony of affection and esteem.

"There may, indeed, be some kind of restraint, some check upon our zeal during the life of the party, from an apprehension that praise might be mistaken for flattery, and that instead of promoting a general sense of the good man's virtue, it might be the means of exposing him to envy. But when a man is dead, praise is less suspected; and those who would have listened very unwillingly to his commendations when living, will be the first to applaud and support it when he is no more. Whatever prejudices he had to combat, whatever opposition was formed to his designs, while he was busy in the pursuit, the man of public spirit is no sooner at rest from his labours and his life (which always end together), than the sentiments of the public are united on his behalf, and all attend with pleasure to the recital of those actions of the dead, which the living will find difficult to imitate.

"The late Captain Thomas Coram, now gone to his grave in a good old age, with the universal regret of the knowing and upright part of mankind, was a person whose merit and virtues were so extraordinary, exerted with such vigour, and with so great constancy for the benefit of society, that an attempt to raise some little monument to his memory, cannot fail of being well received by the public, whose servant he was for upwards of forty years before his death, without any other wages than the honest satisfaction he felt in doing good and discharging his duty; and will, at the same time, furnish a pleasing employment to one who loved him from the contemplation of his singular character, and for that rugged integrity which distinguished him exceedingly in the present age, and which would have done him no small honour even in better times. An abler hand might have easily undertaken the task, but none could perform it with a better will.

"He was born about the year 1668, bred in the sea-service, and spent the first part of his life in the station of master of a vessel trading to our colonies, by which he gained a perfect acquaintance with that commerce which is of so great consequence, and produces so great profit to this nation. He acquired very early, a sincere and warm attachment to the true interests of his country—had a real concern for them, and did not affect public spirit to cover any private views. His experience was his principal guide, and from thence he learned to consider rational liberty, active industry, and unblemished probity, as the only principles upon which national prosperity could be built; and to these, therefore, he gave his loudest voice and his most earnest endeavours. Free from all hypocrisy, he spoke what he thought with vehemence. But his zeal did not rest in words; it was no less visible in his actions: so that not contented with wishing well to his country, and serving it faithfully in his private and particular capacity, he ventured to step out of the common road, and exerted himself in favour of many projects, from no other motive than their being of general utility.

"It may create some wonder, that without any other qualifications than these, Captain Coram should undertake to form schemes considerable for their extent, and very important in their intentions; and still more wonderful that he should procure, from men of great abilities and long acquaintance with business, an approbation of these schemes, and carry them at length into execution, by dint of unwearied application, and a perseverance that nothing could delay, disturb, or destroy. But this he certainly did, and that without any act but that of disclaiming it—without any address beyond that of showing the advantages which the public would reap from his projects—he actually brought them, sooner or later, to bear, is a position so well supported by facts, that, though it is a little improbable, it must be believed.

"But if he wanted certain accomplishments—if he was deficient in some things which are thought necessary to form a successful solicitor, he had certain talents that supplied these defects. He had an honesty that, though it was a little rough, carried such apparent marks of its being genuine, that those who conversed with him but a little, lost all apprehensions of being deceived; and if this did not give him an easier entrance, it certainly procured him an earlier confidence than would have resulted from a more polished behaviour. His arguments were nervous, though not nice—founded commonly upon facts, and the consequences that he drew, so closely connected with them, as to need no further proof than a fair explanation. When once he made an impression, he took care it should not wear out; for he enforced it continually by the most pathetic remonstrances. In short, his logic was plain sense, his eloquence the natural language of the heart.

"When the possession of Nova Scotia was first recovered to the crown of Great Britain by force of arms, and secured afterwards by a treaty of peace, Captain Coram very early saw the consequence that this province was of to the natural interest of this nation and her colonies. He was, therefore, very eager and very earnest to have it thoroughly settled, which, if once done, he very well knew, that the advantages arising from agriculture, fishing, and trade, for which, from the richness of its soil, the convenience of its coasts, and the multiplicity of its harbours, it was admirably adapted, would make the value of it quickly known. In this, if he had not the good fortune he expected and deserved, he was not totally disappointed; and, at the same time, had the pleasure to perceive, that the more his notions were attended to, and the closer they were examined, the plainer and more probable they appeared; so that the utility of his scheme was acknowledged in a much greater degree than was, at that time of day, held expedient to carry it into execution.

"But as plans for the public service, well laid, though they sleep for a long time, seldom fail of waking at last, when, through a train of unlooked-for accidents and unexpected events, administrations are roused to attention, so, before his death, he had the satisfaction of seeing his old scheme revived, and this province, which had been so long neglected, owned and considered in that light in which he had long before placed it. This must certainly have given him great consolation, more especially when he perceived that it was carried on under the auspice of a noble person nearly allied to him in sentiment, and who had no other motive to that care and concern which he has shown for this rising colony but his affection to his country, and to whatever may contribute to strengthen her extensive empire, and secure the continuance of that prosperity which she derives from naval power, and settlements well placed and worthily directed.

"May such noble attempts meet with that success they deserve! May this country, so well situated, be thoroughly peopled and effectually cultivated! May protestants from every climate meet therein with a happy retreat from all kinds of oppression, and, by the help of their own industry, under the protection of the British government, acquire a comfortable assistance, which they will never want spirit to defend!

"He was highly instrumental in promoting another good design—a design equally beneficial to Britain at home, and to British subjects abroad, which coalition of interests is a thing always to be wished, and may, as in this case actually it was, be without much difficulty accomplished. The design here intended was the procuring a bounty upon naval stores imported from the colonies—a matter of vast advantage to the mother country, as it freed her from the necessity of dependence upon foreigners for commodities of essential consequence to her strength, and even to her safety, as it prevented the purchasing them with ready money, which was, in effect, saving so much treasure, and, as it exempted her from many difficulties which she had often felt, and from the apprehension of which she could not otherwise be delivered—points, one would imagine, of so serious a nature, as, if once proposed, to command the strictest attention, and the truth of which, once known, from a close examination, never to be let slip out of memory. The design was likewise of infinite benefit to the colonies, because it afforded the means of enriching them by returns from Britain, which, though nature furnished them with the commodities, they could not otherwise have had. It removed impediments that had long subsisted—it opened a way for improvement, that, though often wished for, could not but with the assistance of this method be attempted; and it converted into value and use, lands and timber that would otherwise have produced nothing. To the inhabitants of the colonies, therefore, there could be nothing more satisfactory—hardly anything so advantageous. But though this is saying a great deal, yet it is not all.

"As salutary and as profitable as this measure might be, considered in these distinct lights, yet its worth was heightened, its importance raised, and its utility demonstrated from another consideration, which was, its uniting the mother country and her daughters in those points of interest which ought to be eminently dear to both. At the same time that it freed Great Britain from depending upon foreigners, it made her sensibly feel the support she received from her plantations; and while the colonies reaped a just return of profit from this assistance, they were, at the same time, more closely connected, and taught to discover the strong and inseparable ties by which they were bound to the mother country. These were the undeniable consequences of Captain Coram's project, and which will do eternal honour to his memory: they were the true and only motives to that ardour with which he pursued it. Enthusiasm was natural to his constitution; but it was a political enthusiasm of the most noble kind—it was that of laying out all his faculties for the public good.

"But we must not imagine, that this gentleman's knowledge of and love for the colonies carried him, in any degree, out of that path which a true Briton ought to tread. He loved the daughters dearly; but he loved them as daughters, and therefore could not brook the least disrespect or disobedience in them towards their parent. The hatters, a very industrious and a very useful body of our manufacturers, thought themselves, with reason, aggrieved by the method taken, in some of the plantations, to interfere with their trade at foreign markets. Captain Coram no sooner heard of this complaint, than he examined it attentively and impartially, and when he perceived that it was founded in right, he espoused it with spirit, he prosecuted it with diligence, and he obtained for that laborious and indefatigable people all the redress they could expect. They would have acknowledged this service by a grateful and handsome return; but Captain Coram had a notion, that if a man's hands were not empty, they could not long be clean: he had a just sense of their gratitude, but did not care to have it expressed by any other present than that of a hat, which he received as often as he had occasion, and which, in its size, spoke the good wishes of the makers in a very legible character.

"In his private life this gentleman showed the same probity, the same cheerfulness, the same frankness, the same warmth, and the same affection that he discovered in matters which respected the public; so that, as a master and as a husband, he acted upon the very same principles that he would have certainly shown if he had been raised to any conspicuous station of life. It is necessary to mention this, that the uniformity of his conduct may appear, which affords the truest method of judging of men's real characters, so as to leave no scruple or doubt upon the minds even of the most cautious enquirers. Beheld in this light, there could not well be conceived a man of greater simplicity of manners. What he thought, he spoke; what he wished, he declared without hesitation, pursued without relaxation or disguise, and never considered obstacles any farther than to discover means to surmount them.

"While he lived in that part of this metropolis which is the common residence of seafaring people, he used to come early into the city, and return late, according as his business required his presence; and both these circumstances afforded him frequent occasions of seeing young children exposed, sometimes alive, sometimes dead, and sometimes dying, which affected him extremely. The reader cannot wonder at this; for a public-spirited man is always humane: and he who is inclined to wear out his life in rendering services to his fellow-subjects, will naturally have the most tender feeling for the sufferings of his fellow-creatures. This was precisely Mr. Coram's case: he saw this calamity in its proper light, and, like an honest and worthy man, thought it would do honour to the nation to show a public spirit of compassion for children thus deserted, through the indigence or cruelty of their parents, and the rather because this was already done in other countries.

"He began, in respect to this design, as he did in all others, with making it the topic of his conversation, that he might learn the sentiments of other men, and from thence form some notion whether what he had in view was practicable. It was not long before he concluded in the affirmative, and, upon frequent trials, he found that there were numbers of all ranks of his sentiments, and not a few who thought it a shame, that a charity so obvious, so useful, and so necessary, should have been so long neglected. This pleased him extremely, and he undertook, with the greatest alacrity possible, to bring so noble, so beneficent, so charitable, so national, and so christian an undertaking to bear, by procuring for it the sanction of public authority. But alas! he found his expectations strangely disappointed by an infinity of cross accidents that would certainly have wearied out the patience of a man whose resolution had not been equal to the vehemence of his temper. To this circumstance Mr. Coram opposed an unrelenting perseverance, arising from a well-founded persuasion, that if the design was not carried into execution by him, it might for a long time, perhaps for ever, remain abortive.

"This laudable, this invincible obstinacy, carried him through seventeen years of labour, which scarce any other man would have supported for seventeen months, if his own private fortune had been the basis of his pursuit. In this space, the opinion of the public had been frequently declared on his side; and several persons of sound sense and enlarged minds actually bequeathed considerable sums to this charity, when it should have a legal authority, which was the highest testimony they could possibly bear of their sense of its utility. Our advocate for the helpless and the unborn left no stone unturned, let no opportunity slip, but continued to solicit where he had no interest, with as much ardour and anxiety as if every deserted child had been his own, and the cause of the unfounded Hospital that of his family. His arguments moved some—the natural humanity of their own temper more—his firm and generous example most of all; for even people of rank began to be ashamed to see a man's hair become grey in the course of a solicitation by which he was to get nothing. Those who did not enter far enough into the case to compassionate the unhappy infants for whom he was a suitor, could not help pitying him, or indeed forbear admiring a virtue so much more worthy of respect, considering the age in which it was exerted—a virtue which would have done honour to the most virtuous nations in the most virtuous periods—a virtue that made an impression even on such as thought it incomprehensible. But however it was, an impression it made, and a general disposition appeared in favour of this charity. It is, however, doubtful what effect this would have had, or how soon that effect might have been produced, if it had any.

"But this good man, whose head was fertile in expedients, bethought himself at last of applying to the ladies. He knew their nature, he knew their influence, and soon found that he was in the right road. They did not listen much to his arguments, for the sweetness of their own tempers supplied a tenderness that rendered arguments unnecessary. They concurred with Mr. Coram in his design, and they concurred in his own way. They were earnest, assiduous, and sincere, and manifested a greater eagerness to do good than the most self-interested dare avow in pursuits upon their own account. This answered its end; and, by the help of these auxiliaries, Mr. Coram was enabled to procure a charter, to prevent the most infamous of all murders, because the most unnatural, and which will supply thousands of useful subjects to the crown of Great Britain—a charter which did honour to the great seal, and spoke, in a literal sense, that prince whose stamp it bore—the father of his people, as he was before confessed in every other sense whatever.

"On Tuesday, November 20th, 1739, was held at Somerset House, the first general meeting of the nobility and gentry appointed by his Majesty's royal charter to be Governors and Guardians of the Hospital for the maintenance and education of exposed and deserted young children, to hear their charter read, and to appoint their Secretary and a Committee. Previous to the reading of the charter, Captain Coram, the petitioner for the charter, addressed his Grace the Duke of Bedford, the President, in the following manner:—

"'My Lord Duke of Bedford,

'It is with inexpressible pleasure I now present your Grace, at the head of this noble and honourable corporation, with his Majesty's royal charter, for establishing an Hospital for exposed children, free of all expense, through the assistance of some compassionate great ladies, and other good persons.

'I can, my lord, sincerely aver, that nothing would have induced me to embark in a design so ful of difficulties and discouragements, but a zeal for the service of his Majesty, in preserving the lives of great numbers of his innocent subjects.

'The long and melancholy experience of this nation has too demonstrably shewn, with what barbarity tender infants have been exposed and destroyed, *for want of proper means of preventing the disgrace, and succouring the necessities of their parents.*

'The charter will disclose the extensive nature and end of this Charity, in much stronger terms than

I can possibly pretend to describe them, so that I have only to thank your Grace and many other noble personages, for all that favourable protection which hath given life and spirit to my endeavours.

'My Lord, although my declining years will not permit me to hope seeing the full accomplishment of my wishes, yet I can now rest satisfied, and it is what I esteem an ample reward of more than seventeen years expensive labour and steady application, that I see your Grace at the head of this charitable trust, assisted by so many noble and honourable Governors.

'Under such powerful influences and directions, I am confident of the final success of my endeavours, and that the public will one day reap the happy and lasting fruits of your Grace's and this Corporation's measures, and as long as my life and poor abilities endure, I shall not abate of my zealous wishes and most active services for the good and prosperity of this truly noble and honourable Corporation.' "

"After the charter was read, Dr. Mead, in the most pathetic manner, set forth the necessity of such an Hospital, and the vast advantages that must accrue to the nation by this useful establishment, which was received with universal approbation, because nobody could entertain the least doubt of the truth or certainty of what the Doctor said.

"At a subsequent Court, the same learned person moved, that the thanks of the Corporation might be given to Mr. Thomas Coram, for his indefatigable and successful applications in favour of this charity, which otherwise would have wanted a legal foundation. It may be easily supposed, that the good old man was not insensible on receiving the only reward of which his labours were capable. But he was just, as well as generous, and would not take more to himself than he deserved. He therefore desired that the thanks of the Corporation might be likewise given to the ladies,* through whose assistance his own endeavours became effectual, and he was accordingly empowered to return them the thanks of that honourable body, which was an additional pleasure to a mind sincere and grateful like his.

"Time and accidents could make but little alteration in his temper. The motives from which he first espoused this charity, kept him always attached to its interests; he often visited the Hospital, and saw the children rescued from misery by his care and compassion, with as much pleasure and tenderness as if they had been his own, as indeed in some sense they were. He beheld the lists of benefactors with more pleasure than a miser regards those of his securities. He had the same delight in perceiving the

---

* Even in the case of the "ladies" he had sometimes to encounter difficulties. Attached to a memorial addressed "To H. R. H. the Princess Amelia," now lodged at the Hospital, is the following note:—

"On Innocent's Day, the 28th of December, 1737, I went to St. James's Palace to present this petition, having been advised first to address the lady of the bed-chamber in waiting to introduce it. But the Lady Isabella Finch, who was the lady in waiting, gave me very rough words, and bid me be gone with my petition, which I did, without opportunity of presenting it."

quick progress of this excellent establishment, as a man of another turn would have felt from the improvement of his own estate. This was peculiar to his character—this was the ruling passion of his mind—this was the elixir that kept him from feeling the frowns of fortune in the winter of his age. Wrapt in that cloak of public spirit, which, though worn for so many years, never grew threadbare, he heard those storms whistle around him, unmoved, which would have frighted a person of ordinary courage out of his wits.

"For the truth is, honest reader, and I must not conceal it, that this worthy man, who could feel so much for others, felt but little for himself. After he lost his wife, the only loss for which he ever showed much regret, he was so attentive to public affairs, as to be a little too careless of his own, insomuch, that he might have known even this evil, which no man could have known, while it was in his power to relieve. But his friend Mr. Gideon, who loved him for loving the public, interposed, and obtained a subscription for his comfortable support, towards which, His Royal Highness the late Prince of Wales subscribed twenty guineas per annum, and paid it with as much punctuality as any of the rest of the subscribers, who were most of them merchants; and upon this friendly assistance which he lived to want, but not to ask, he subsisted for some time, which gave him an opportunity to form new schemes of the same kind with those he had executed already; schemes full of goodness, and which had a tendency to spread the influence of Britain, and to expand the nation's glory in the like degree.

"The reader may be surprised—and indeed his surprise will be very excusable—that a person whose worth and services were so well known should be left to such distress, and that in a country where the public pays so much to place-men, no notice should be taken of a man who deserved a place so well as Mr. Coram did. But first of all, it must be considered, that though the public discharge the expense of many, yet their choice is asked in filling very few places. Our hero had, indeed, very great qualities, but they were far from being well turned for any thing of this kind. He who had spent his life in soliciting for others, could not speak a word for himself. It is therefore no wonder that he was not provided for. Dumb men are not fit for places. But if the reader enquires why he did not speak, the answer, perhaps, may not be difficult. Men of true public spirit are, of all others, the most ashamed to ask private favours. In others it would be pride, in them it is the effect of principle. It may be said, then, a place should have been given him. To this there can be no reply; yet, perhaps, it may be some excuse to say, that, while a multitude of claims are put in for every place, we have no reason to be amazed, that a man who would never ask should always be forgot.

"But Providence provided for him, and he had a comfortable subsistence to the last, by a method that he did not, nor indeed could take amiss. He

Fac-Simile of Captn. Coram's Autograph, when 81 Years Old, then petitioning the Government to found an Establishment for the Education of Indian Girls.

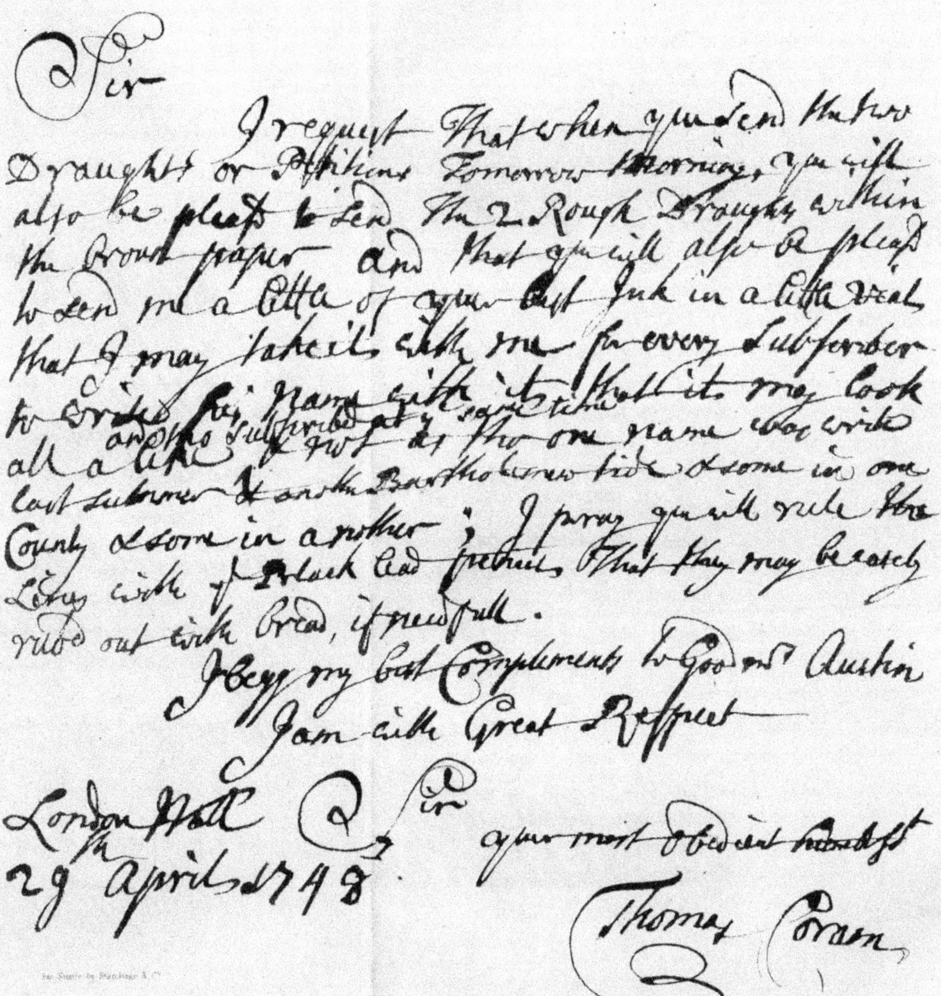

Sir

I request That when you Send the two Draughts or Petitions Tomorrow Morning, you will also be pleased to Send the 2 Rough Draughts within the Brown paper And that you will also be pleased to send me a little of your best Ink in a little Vial, that I may take it with me for every Subscriber to Write his Name with it, that it may look all a like, & not as tho one name was writ [another subscribed at ye same time] last Summer & another Bartholomew tide & some in one County & some in another; I pray you will rule the Lines with ye Black lead pencils That they may be easely rubbed out with Bread, if needfull.

I beg my best Complements to Good Mrs Austin

I am with Great Respect

Sir

your most Obedient humble Servt

Thomas Coram

London Wall 29th April 1748

Fac-Simile by Standidge & Co

The material originally positioned here is too large for reproduction in this reissue. A PDF can be downloaded from the web address given on page iv of this book, by clicking on 'Resources Available'.

was maintained by the voluntary subscription* of men of public spirit: this was an honour to them, and an honour to him. Had his distress been generally known, he might, no doubt, have been more amply provided for; but this was what he did not want, and what he would never seek. He was content with a little—pleased with being his own master, and with having the liberty to employ his thoughts, to the end of his life, in the same manner that they had been employed from the beginning—in contriving for the public benefit; for whatever his circumstances were, his heart could never be narrow.

"His last design, now left an orphan to the public care, which it well deserves, was a scheme for uniting the Indians in North America more closely to the British interest, by an establishment for the education of Indian girls. This is, indeed, a very political contrivance; for if the girls be brought up in Christian principles, we have just grounds to hope—indeed, we have no reason to doubt—that the Indian children, of both sexes, in the next generation, will be brought up Christians. This would be

* On Dr. Brocklesby applying to Captain Coram, to know whether a subscription being opened for his benefit would not offend him, he received this noble answer:—"I have not wasted the little wealth of which I was formerly possessed in self-indulgence and vain expenses, and am not ashamed to confess that, in this my old age, I am poor."

Upon the death of Coram, this pension was continued to poor old Leveridge, for whose volume of songs Hogarth had, in 1727, engraved a title-page and frontispiece, and who, at the age of ninety, had scarcely any other prospect than that of a parish subsistence.—*J. Ireland.*

a refined stroke of policy; for he is the wisest and ablest of all politicians who, by promoting the glory of God, interests the Divine Providence in extending the power of any nation. We know in how wonderful a manner the gospel was propagated; and we may confidently expect, that where this is sincerely the aim of any government, the same assistance will not be wanting: for whatever men may do, the great Author of all things never alters his maxims, and to follow them is the most infallible method of securing, might we not say commanding, success. May this charitable and pious purpose, in which he lived long enough to make some progress, be completed in virtue of his proposal; and let the benighted Indians in America join with the deserted Foundlings in Britain in blessing the memory of this worthy man, by whom a provision was made that they should come to the knowledge of truth, and of the means of making themselves happy here by their industry, and by their piety, hereafter.

"If it had been in our power to have taken notice of all the other instances he gave of beneficence, fortitude, and love for society, which are the true virtues of a patriot, this little work would swell to a volume. What is here said, therefore, must be regarded as an imperfect and hasty sketch of his character, which however may, from its intention, rather than performance, be agreeable to his friends, and may perhaps serve, in some measure, to excite in others a desire of imitating so amiable an example; for who that has any respect for virtue, any appetite to laudable and spotless fame—the noblest purchase that human industry can make—can be insensible to that just and general concern which the best and worthiest men in this metropolis have shown for the loss of Captain Coram, or that readiness with which they have expressed their approbation of his conduct, and the voluntary testimonies they have given to his merit and services. These are things that will affect those who are above the common pursuits of the world, who seek not either tinsel grandeur or the embarrassment of riches, but yet are far from leading a life of indolence, or disclaiming all pretensions to that glory which is so properly the reward of virtue, that it can attend on nothing else.

"This singular and memorable man exchanged this life for a better, and passed from doing to enjoying good, on Friday, March 29th, 1751, in the fourscore and fourth year of his age, making it his last request, that his corpse might be interred in the Chapel of the Foundling Hospital, which shows he had that excellent foundation at his heart, when all things that regarded this world besides were out of his thoughts—a circumstance that demonstrates the steadiness of his affection, and the happiness he had of what he had done for this place, when he was on the point of going where pious and charitable actions afford the highest recommendations—where his merit in that and in all other respects will be fully known and fully rewarded.

"Accordingly, on Wednesday, the 3rd of April, agreeable to his request, his remains were interred in the Chapel of this Hospital, his pall supported by six, and his funeral attended by a great number of the honourable and worthy persons who are Governors of this useful charity, and who manifested, upon this melancholy occasion, that sincere regard for the deceased, and the pleasure they took in paying this deserved respect to his memory — a ceremony which, joined to the high reputation and numerous acquaintance of the deceased, could not have failed of attracting abundance of public-spirited persons, desirous of giving this last mark of their esteem for a man of Mr. Coram's worth, and who, through the progress of a long life, had shown himself a laudable as well as active member of society.

"But the concourse was much increased, and the solemnity of the funeral greatly heightened, by the voluntary appearance of the choir of St. Paul's Cathedral, who were at the Hospital, ready in their surplices to receive the body, and who performed, with the universal approbation of a crowded and distinguished audience, a grave and noble piece of music, suitable to the sad occasion, and which, with the genuine testimonies of sorrow, not to be suppressed, did all the honour to this good man that even the piety and affection of his friends could expect. The Governors of the Hospital have it also in their intention to raise a suitable monument, though, indeed, the Hospital itself may be so styled, that posterity may be the better acquainted with his virtues, and their gratitude.

"Let me be permitted to conclude, with what

may add some degree of merit to this little piece, deficient enough in other respects, the words made use of by a friend of his, in the paragraph which gave the first hint to this performance, and which is, indeed, a true character of Mr. Thomas Coram in very few words :—

"'*That when others are remembered by titles and adulations, his shall be nobler fame to have lived above the fear of everything but an unworthy action.*'"

The following Inscription, cut in stone, is placed in the southern arcade of the Chapel.

"CAPTAIN THOMAS CORAM,

whose name will never want a monument
so long as this Hospital shall subsist,
was born in the year 1668;
a man eminent in that most eminent virtue,
the love of mankind;
little attentive to his private fortune,
and refusing many opportunities of increasing it,
his time and thoughts were continually employed
in endeavours to promote the public happiness,
both in this kingdom and elsewhere;
particularly in the Colonies of North America;
and his endeavours were many times crowned
with the desired success.

His unwearied solicitation, for above seventeen years together,
(which would have baffled the patience and industry
of any man less zealous in doing good)
and his application to persons of distinction, of both sexes,
obtained at length the Charter of the Incorporation,
(bearing date the 17th of October, 1739,)
for the maintenance and education
of exposed and deserted young children,
by which many thousands of lives
may be preserved to the public, and employed in a frugal
and honest course of industry.

He died the 29th March, 1751, in the 84th year of his age ;
poor in worldly estate, rich in good works .
and was buried, at his own desire, in the Vault underneath this
Chapel (the first there deposited) at the east end thereof,
many of the governors and other gentlemen
attending the funeral to do honour to his memory.

Reader,

Thy actions will shew whether thou art sincere
in the praises thou may'st bestow on him ;
and if thou hast virtue enough to commend his virtues,
forget not to add also the imitation of them."

PORTRAIT OF THOMAS EMMERSON, Esq.,

(A Governor and most liberal Contributor)

By HIGHMORE.

Of whom an account has already been given.

A LARGE SEA-PEICE,

(Representing the English Fleet in the Downs)

By MONAMY.

Monamy, who was a good painter of sea-pieces, was born in Jersey, and from his circumstances, or the views of his family, had little reason to expect the fame he afterwards acquired; having received his first rudiments of drawing from a sign and house-painter on London Bridge. But when nature gives real talents, they break forth in the homeliest school. The shallow waves that rolled under his window taught young Monamy what his master could not teach him, and fitted him to imitate the turbulence of the ocean. In Painters' Hall is a large piece by him, painted in 1726. He died at his house in Westminster, the beginning of 1749.

THE CARTOON OF THE MURDER OF THE INNOCENTS,

By RAFFAEL.

This cartoon came into the possession of the Hospital by the conditional bequest of Prince Hoare, Esq., as follows:—

"I direct that my cartoon painted by Raffaelli, representing the Murder of the Innocents, be offered by my executors, hereinafter named, to the President and Council of the Royal Academy of Arts, for sale at the price of two thousand pounds, and if they should decline becoming the purchasers at that price wholly, or should not purchase it within six months after it be offered to them, Then I direct my executors to offer it to the Directors of the National Gallery at the price of four thousand pounds, and if they should decline to purchase it at that sum wholly, or should not purchase it within twelve months after it has been so offered to them—

"Then I will and direct, that the said cartoon be presented either to the *Foundling Hospital*, or to a Public Hall or College, according to the decision of my friends the said Samuel Prado, and Sharon Turner, and Mr. Howard, the Secretary of the Royal Academy, or the decision of any two of them."

The Council of the Royal Academy of Arts, and the Directors of the National Gallery, having declined purchasing the cartoon upon the terms stated, it was then presented to the Hospital by the Trustees named in Mr. Hoare's will.

The late lamented painter, B. R. Haydon, in a letter to the Secretary of the Hospital, dated 3rd October, 1837, has given the following graphical account of this picture:—

"Dear Sir,

"I was extremely gratified yesterday at having ocular demonstration by your kindness, that one of the finest instances in the world of variety of expression and beauty of composition, as a work of 'high art,' was out of danger and secure: I allude to the centre part of one of the last cartoons which belonged to the set executed by Raffael, at the order of Leo X., and sent afterwards to Flanders, to be executed in tapestry, for the purpose of increasing the splendour of those exhibitions, so well known in Rome during Lent, at the Vatican.

"The original number was thirteen; but, in consequence of the Flemish weavers cutting them into slips for their working machinery, after the tapestry was executed and sent to Rome, the original cartoons were left mingled together, without care or interest, in boxes.

"When Rubens was in England, he told Charles I. the condition they were in; and the king, who had the finest taste, desired him to procure them. Seven perfect ones were purchased, all, it may be inferred, which remained, and sent to his Majesty: what became, or had become of the remainder, nobody knows; but here and there, all over Europe, fragments have appeared. At Oxford there are two or three heads; and, I believe, the Duke of Hamilton or Buccleuch have others. But this sublime fragment, possessed by the Governors, is certainly the largest portion of those which are last remaining. I am quite sure, on this explanation, the Governors will perceive, on every point of view, the value, both as property and as a work of art, of this invaluable composition. After the king's misfortunes, the cartoons now at Hampton Court were sold, with the rest of his Majesty's fine collection; but by Cromwell's express order, they were bought in for three hundred pounds.

"During the reign of Charles II., they were offered to France for fourteen thousand francs, but Charles was dissuaded from selling them. I cannot give you my authority at the moment.

"This portion of the Murder of the Innocents was sold at Westminster as disputed property. Prince Hoare's father, before the sale, explained to an opulent friend the great treasure about to be disposed of, and persuaded him to advance the money requisite, on condition of sharing the property. To his great wonder, he bought it for twenty-six pounds, and his friend, having no taste, told Mr. Hoare, if he would paint him and his family, he would relinquish his right.

"I had these particulars from Prince Hoare, (his son) who repeatedly told me. I took Canova to see it (1815), who was enthusiastic in admiration; and I was allowed, in my early studies (1804), thirty-three years ago, to copy all the heads, and I am quite sure there is hardly a day passes in which I do not feel the great advantage of so sublime a model for expression and composition. Look at the villain in front, grappling the leg of a victim child, and rolling on like a mountain fragment, which nothing can arrest! while the fiery and passionate mother throttles the monster to save her child, though you can perceive the mere physical weight of the iron-faced murderer will render her feminine resistance useless and in vain!

"As an instance of preserving *beauty* in violent expression, this head is unequalled in any of the great works of art in the world. It is a model of study, and I remember nothing to be compared to it.

"Above this group is a woman of phlegmatic nature, as a contrast to the violent temperament of the one below; she is pale, blank, and utterly unnerved; she stares at the murderer, who is pressing down the innocent face of her infant, and dashing the dagger into its throat, quite paralyzed and unable to resist. Above her is a young mother, with long hair, tenderly protecting her child, while the group is finished by a scoundrel, who, holding the hair of one that is trying to escape, stabs the infant of the opposite woman, who has her hand in his eyes.

"For all the intricate beauties of composition, for various modifications of the same feeling, according to the character chosen, there is no finer example any where, and such a work ought not to be in a back room badly lighted and scarcely seen, but in a room by itself, well lighted, the walls coloured on purpose, and in fact, such a production for the sake of the art, should be shewn off to every advantage. It would be justice to Raffael, an honor to the Hospital and its Governors, and a kind compliment to my late friend: it would do the English school great good, and advance the taste of all classes.

"One day in the week an advanced student, under proper introduction, might be admitted to finish his studies from it, and it might always be regularly shewn and explained to the visitors.

"Pray, my dear Sir, lay my letter before the Governors, if you think it would not be a liberty, at their next meeting, and be assured I have no other object but the good of the art, the tenderest respect for my late friend, and an earnest desire to see so valuable a prize preserved as long as the materials will hold together.

"I am, dear Sir,
"With every apology,
"Truly yours,
"B. R. HAYDON."

"To M. Lievesley, Esq."

The Governors of the Hospital have since sent

this valuable cartoon, by way of loan, to the Directors of the National Gallery, for exhibition to the public, where it may now be seen to advantage, the Directors having been at considerable expense in restoring it, and securing it against damage for the future.*

Mr. Prince Hoare, the donor of this work of art to the Hospital, was author of various dramatic and other writings. He was born and educated at Bath, and instructed in painting by his father, William Hoare, one of the original members of the Royal Academy. He went to Italy for the further acquirement of his art, and studied at Rome, under Mengs; but after his return, through infirm health, declined the profession. The following are his dramatic productions, of which a few only are published:—"Julia, or, Such Things Were—tragedy; Indiscretion; Sighs, or the Daughter; The Partners—comedies; No Song, No Supper; The Cave of Trophonius; Dido; The Prize; My Grandmother; Three and the Deuce; Lock and Key; Mahmoud; The Friend in Need; The Captive of Spilberg; Italian Villagers; Chains of the Heart—musical pieces."

In consequence of succeeding, in 1799, to the honorary appointment of Secretary for Foreign Correspondence to the Royal Academy, he published "Academic Annals of Painting, Sculpture, and Architecture," a work since continued by the academy

* Mr. Kinton, an old friend and one of the executors of Mr. Hoare, was elected a Governor in consequence of the bequest of the above cartoon.

at successive periods; and, shortly afterwards, "An Inquiry into the Requisite Cultivation and Present State of the Arts of Design in England." "The Artist," a collection of essays, written chiefly by professional persons (to which he contributed several papers), is edited by him.

In 1813, he published "Epochs of Art," containing historical observations on the uses and progress of painting and sculpture. This last work is dedicated to the Prince Regent. He is author of a little piece entitled, "Love's Victims," and some tracts of a moral tendency.

Besides the works above enumerated, Mr. Prince Hoare, in 1820, published "Memoirs of the late Granville Sharpe, Esq.," a gentleman universally esteemed for his learning, piety, and political rectitude.

In the year 1825 he published a tract, entitled, "Easter; a Companion to the Book of Common Prayer." This small but valuable work is a manual explanatory of all the Latin words and phrases, and other appropriate terms of the church service, with other matters essential to the due comprehension of its important subject. In this interesting and learned work, which would do honour to any ecclesiastical authority, he has modestly suppressed his name, and published it under the simple designation of "A Layman."

The following communication has been made to the compiler, by his friend Morris Lievesley, Esq., who has been officially connected with the Hospital more than half a century:—

"Foundling Hospital, 1st Jan. 1847.

"My dear Mr. Brownlow,

"I have much pleasure in complying with your request, that I would communicate to you, for the work you have in hand, such anecdotes connected with this Institution as were either related to me by my predecessors in office, or to which I myself have been a party; and I do it the more cheerfully, feeling that being admitted into your pages, (however trifling their character) they will obtain that notice which I consider them deserving of.

"I remain my dear Mr. Brownlow,

"Yours faithfully,

"Morris Lievesley."

Elijah raising the Son of the Widow.—This picture was submitted to sale by auction under the auspices of the then celebrated Mr. Langford, who, finding there were no bidders—probably from its being a portion of a large picture, said, "Gentlemen, if you will allow me, I will bid ten guineas for it, and withdraw the lot, upon the understanding that I may be permitted to make a donation of it to the Foundling Hospital."

Suffer Little Children to come unto Me.—This picture, from a want of tone in the colouring, has not received the encomium which, in other respects, it merits. Mr. West, the late President of the Royal Academy, having one day attentively examined it, and being informed of the public opinion regarding it, observed, "that may be true, but I never saw a picture exhibiting finer and more correct drawing of limbs. It should be sent to the Royal Academy, for the younger artists to study from."

Altar-Piece.—This picture has been twice re-touched by the artist, indeed nearly re-painted. On its being finally placed in its present position, Mr. West observed to the Secretary, who was standing by his side, "I knew nothing of harmony in colouring until I re-painted this picture; it stands now one of my best class of works, and you are at liberty to say I said so;" then taking the Secretary by the arm, Mr. West placed him in a position, saying, "this is the focal distance to view it—remember that."

When the Arch-Duke Nicholas (the present Emperor of Russia), with his brother the Arch-Duke Michael, visited the Foundling Hospital, he gave much attention to the altar-piece, and was placed at the precise focal distance laid down by Mr. West. Having looked at the picture some minutes, the Arch-Duke Nicholas observed to the Secretary, who was in waiting upon the Royal visitors and their suite, that there was a stain upon the face of Christ which should be attended to, and instantly mounting the communion table, and touching with his finger a clot of paint in the centre of the forehead he found it soft and oozing, and requested that Mr. West might be immediately informed of the discovery. Mr. West attended, and had the picture removed to his studio. When it was returned and replaced in its frame, the artist, addressing the Secretary, said, "I will tell you all about it. Sir Joseph Banks introduced to the Society a new fish oil which he recommended to be used by all artists. I fell into his notions, and painted with fish oil some of my best pictures, but the d—d oil will not dry—no dryer will do—scraping will not do unless you scrape the canvass also. D—n the fellow, he has given me more trouble than all the fish oil in the world is worth. I now mix all my colours in my own house; I will not even trust * * * * *."

Sea-Piece.—Taylor White, Esq., then Treasurer of the Foundling, having purchased several small Sea-pieces at a broker's shop in Fleet Market, was induced, on finding a succession of similar pictures from the same pencil offered for sale, to enquire for the name and condition of the artist; and after much difficulty he ascertained the name to be Brooking, and that he resided in a garret of the house belonging to the broker. In consequence of an interview between Mr. White and Brooking, the latter was encouraged to paint the sea-piece in question in one of the rooms of the Institution, his garret not affording sufficient space. The picture was painted in eighteen days, and its merits are supposed not to be surpassed by any other marine painter.

Moses and Pharaoh's Daughter.—The celebrated John Wilkes, when a young man, was elected a Governor of the Foundling. At a meeting of the General Court, a question was mooted which threatened protracted debate, when Mr. Wilkes, who was then almost unknown amongst his colleagues, rose and said, "I see no difficulty in the matter at issue. The question is this—Are the benefits of this charity to be limited to children who are exposed and deserted—that is, left naked on Salisbury Plain? I maintain that a mother dying from want, with her infant at her breast, that infant falls within the view of the charter. Are we living under the dispensations of Christianity, and yet cripple our notions of charity?"—then, turning to the picture—"If so," continued he, "let us fall back upon ancient times, and take a lesson from the heathen maid."

THE CHAPEL.

The Chapel was erected, by subscription, in the year 1747, on the original plan by Mr. Jacobsen, forming the central feature of the north and south fronts of the Hospital building.

Its frontage was then limited in extent to the five middle divisions of the open arcades, and the elevation of the superstructure being detached from the main buildings on each side, presented more distinctness of character in itself, and was advantageous in its effect to the general design of the building. The lower part, or ground plan of the Chapel, was thus isolated by a continued arched corridor, forming a sub-structure for the extension of the upper part, which, on the north and south sides, became a portion of the original building, and was subsequently extended over the east and west ends.

The lower area of the building continues of the original extent, its enclosure forming the appropriate basement of a regular colonnade and entablature of the Ionic order, raised on pedestals, with intermediate continued balustrade, enclosing the front of the sittings in the upper part of the building throughout.

A coved ceiling, of handsome design, springing from the entablature of the colonnade, extends over the central area, or main division of the building, with enriched bands and pendants on its soffite, and the ceilings of the side and east-end divisions are enriched by soffites and arched bands, of appropriate unity of design with the architecture of the colonnade.

The west end is entirely appropriated to the occupation of the children, and for the organ and choir; and from a late alteration, by the removal of part of the original construction, and entire new arrangement of the seats and of the choir, the effect of the general distribution has been much improved, by its suitable distinctness, without interfering with the general uniformity.

The design and effect of the interior of this building is admitted to be striking and impressive; and as an instance of the mode of distribution of so large a portion of the congregation, at an upper level, with pleasing uniformity and picturesque architectural effect, without the disfigurement generally attendant upon galleries, under the most favourable circumstances; it may be considered a specimen of some originality, and worthy of observation. Some alteration and improvement of the details of the style and decoration of the interior, was probably made at the period of the extension of this building, and the windows at the eastern end filled with stained glass. This enrichment has lately been extended also to the windows on the south front.

The panelling on the sides of the lower area, forming the basement of the colonnade, being of regular design and suitable proportions for pictures, would, at this favourable period for the advancement of fresco painting, become peculiarly appropriate for a partial, if not entire application of them for sacred subjects, after the great masters, and congenial to the spirit and advancement of the British art, and the distinguished artists that fostered the original establishment of the charity.

The simple and appropriate distinction given to the divisions of panelling immediately connected with the altar-table, on the east side, could always be continued to be maintained.* The cost of the erection of the Chapel was £6,490.

The advertisement inviting subscribers set forth, "that the Governors being earnestly desirous that the children under their care should be early instructed in the principles of religion and morality, and having no place of public worship to which the children and servants of the Hospital could conveniently resort, have resolved to erect a Chapel adjoining to their Hospital; but that no part of the revenue of the said Hospital which is or shall be given for the support of the children, may be diverted from that use: and in order to defray the expense of erecting the said Chapel, they have opened a subscription for that purpose."

His Majesty George II. subscribed £2,000 towards the erection, and afterwards £1,000 towards supplying a preacher in the Chapel, to instruct the children in the Christian religion, and for other incidental expenses.

---

* This architectural description has been kindly furnished by Joseph Kay, Esq., who has been, for nearly half a century, the architect and surveyor of the Hospital and its estates.

Handel.

Handel, as if influenced by a kindred feeling with Hogarth (for genius is ever noble and generous), very soon engaged in the work of charity at this popular institution. On the 4th May, 1749, he attended the committee at the Hospital, and offered a performance of vocal and instrumental music, the money arising therefrom to be applied towards the finishing of the Chapel.

This performance is thus alluded to in the "Gentleman's Magazine" of that month:—

"The Prince and Princess of Wales, with a great number of persons of quality and distinction, were at the Chapel of the Foundling Hospital, to hear several pieces of vocal and instrumental music composed by George Frederick Handel, Esq., for the benefit of the foundation. 1st. The music of the late Fire Works, and the anthem on the Peace: 2nd. Select pieces from the oratorio of Solomon, relating to the dedication of the temple: and 3rd. Several pieces composed for the occasion, the words taken from scripture, and applicable to the charity and its benefactors. There was no collection, but the tickets were at half-a-guinea, and the audience above a thousand."

For this act of benevolence on the part of Handel, he was immediately enrolled as one of the Governors and Guardians of the Hospital.

During every year after this, until his infirmity obliged him to relinquish his profession, he superintended personally the performance of his matchless

Oratorio of the Messiah, in the Chapel, which netted to the Treasury of the Charity no less a sum than £7000.

The Governors of the Hospital seeing the profitableness of this performance, and being (as it appeared) misinformed of Handel's intention regarding the copyright, prepared a petition to Parliament to secure it for themselves. The latter part of this petition is as follows:—

"That in order to raise a further sum for the benefit of the said charity, George Frederick Handel, Esq., hath been charitably pleased to give to this corporation a composition of musick, called 'The Oratorio of the Messiah,' composed by him the said George Frederick Handel, reserving to himself the liberty only of performing the same for his own benefit during his life: and whereas the said benefaction cannot be secured to the sole use of your petitioners except by the authority of Parliament, your petitioners, therefore, humbly pray, that leave may be given to bring in a bill for the purposes aforesaid."

Upon one of the Governors waiting upon the musician with this form of petition, he soon discovered that the committee of the Hospital had built upon a wrong foundation; for Handel, bursting into a rage, exclaimed—"Te Deivel! for vat sal de Foundling put mein oratorio in de Parlement? Te Deivel! mein music sal not go to de Parlement!"

Here the matter dropped, never to be revived. At the completion of the Chapel, Handel presented the Governors with an organ, and other liberal contributions fell in on the same occasion.

The Communion plate was presented by a Governor, who desired to be "unknown;" and the king's upholsterer gave the velvets for the pulpit, &c.

The Governors of the Hospital felt, naturally enough, a deep affection and veneration for Handel; and therefore, when, in April, 1753, a foolish paragraph appeared in the daily papers, stating, that he was preparing a funeral anthem, to be performed in the Chapel of the Hospital after his death, the Committee desired their Secretary to acquaint him, "That the said paragraph has given this Committee great concern, they being highly sensible that all well-wishers to this charity must be desirous for the continuance of his life, who has been and is so great and generous a benefactor thereto."

With the full concurrence of Handel, the Governors appointed his amanuensis and assistant, Mr. John Christopher Smith, the first organist of the Chapel.

At the death of Handel, it was found he had made the following bequest:—"I give a fair copy of the score, and all the parts of my oratorio called 'The Messiah,' to the Foundling Hospital." The Governors resolved, in grateful memory of their friend and benefactor, to have a dirge and funeral anthem performed in the Chapel, on the 26th May, 1759, on the occasion of his demise, which performance took place under the direction of the organist of the Chapel, Mr. John Christopher Smith.

Benjamin West, R.A.

Mention has been already made, that, on the finishing of the Chapel, Chevalier Casali presented the Governors with an altar-piece, the subject being "The Offering of the Wise Men." This picture occupied its appropriate place till 1801, when two of the Vice-Presidents, John Wilmot, Esq., and Thomas Everett, Esq., M.P., together with Sir Thomas Bernard, Bart., (the Treasurer) and John Puget, Esq., agreed to purchase and present to the Hospital a picture by West, namely—*Christ presenting a little Child.** This picture had been in the hands of a party, by whose mismanagement it had suffered some injury, and therefore West, in his determination to make it fully acceptable to the Governors, almost entirely repainted it. "The care" (he says) "with which I have passed that picture, I flatter myself has now placed it in the first class of pictures from my pencil; at least, I have the satisfaction to find that to be the sentiment of the judges of painting who have seen it."

For this act of generosity, the Governors resolved to elect West one of their corporate body.

He appears to have been highly flattered by this compliment, and in acknowledging it, states that his professional duties will not permit him to become an

---

* "And Jesus called a little child unto him, and set him in the midst of them,

"And said, Verily I say unto you, Except ye be converted, and become as little children, ye shall not enter into the kingdom of heaven.

"And whoso shall receive one such little child in my name, receiveth me."

active member of the Corporation, but to shew his respect and good wishes for the establishment in the only way he could make a return, he intended to add to the embellishments of the Chapel as follows:—

"There are" (he says), "on each side the place of Communion in the Chapel, opposite the Governors' and Governors' Ladies' seats, two panels, well calculated to receive paintings. If the Governors will concur, at my leisure I propose to paint two pictures from sacred history to fill those panels, which I shall beg the Corporation to accept of, as a mark of my respect for the Institution, at the same time, to ask of them the exclusive right of having prints taken from those pictures."

It need not be added that the Governors immediately accepted this munificent and charitable offer, but it is to be lamented that the leisure of the artist never arrived, and that the work remains undone. If perchance any modern artist should read this and have a laudable desire to establish his fame, he cannot do better than carry out the intention of West.

In 1816, the Chapel being then under repair, West had the Altar-Piece taken to his house and again re-touched it, returning it to its place with strong expressions towards this favourite work of his hand.

The Governors had been early taught by Handel, that their Chapel (which was built for the exclusive use of the children and household), was capable of being converted into a source of pecuniary means for increasing the usefulness of the work they had in hand. What Handel began, other eminent musicians continued, and the Governors having received several blind children into the establishment (during the general and indiscriminate admission), they were instructed in music, and became a fruitful source of advantage to the funds of the Charity.* For nearly one hundred years the Chapel has been established, and if the taste of the public for sacred music has increased, and that taste has any beneficial influence on the minds of the people, this Chapel has been one of the humble instruments for effecting it.

The expenses for supporting the Chapel are very considerable, and the only return is from the pew rents and contributions of the public at the Chapel doors.

THE CATACOMBS.

Beneath the Chapel are capacious Vaults, in which were deposited, in 1751, the remains of the Founder, at his own request; since which many of the Governors have also been buried here. The coffins, which are of lead, are enclosed in stone catacombs. Amongst the departed, who were dis-

* There are those remaining of the present generation who, doubtless, recollect Mr. Grenville (the organist), Mr. Printer, Miss Thetford, and "Jenny Freer" (the singers), *all blind Foundlings*, whose talents were much appreciated by the public; by the exercise of which, the expense bestowed upon these orphans in infancy and youth was returned fifty-fold into the coffers of the charity!

tinguished for their zeal in the cause of the Charity, within whose walls they now rest, the following may be specially noticed, viz. :—

1803.—*The Rev. Samuel Harper, M. A.* Thirty-six years Chaplain and afterwards a Governor of the Hospital. He was also one of the Under Librarians of the British Museum.

1807.—*William George Sibley, Esq.* Many years Treasurer of the Honourable East India Company. (*Jane Amphillis,* his wife, is buried in the same vault.)

1808.—*Anthony Van Dam, Esq.*

1810.—*Thomas Everett, Esq., M. P.* A most active Vice-President of the Hospital. By his personal zeal he collected several thousands of pounds for the Charity. (*Martha,* his wife, is also buried in the same vault.)

1813.—*Michael Heathcote, Esq.* A Vice-President.

1818.—*William Watson, Esq., F.R.S.* Serjeant-at-Arms, Attendant on the Great Seal and the House of Lords. Chairman of the Sessions for Middlesex and Westminster. Senior Common Pleader of the City of London, and a Vice-President of the Hospital. (*Susanna,* his wife, is buried in the same vault.)

1818.—*Sir Thomas Bernard, Baronet.* Eleven years Treasurer of the Hospital, and afterwards a

Vice-President.* (*Lady Margaret,* and *Lady Charlotte Matilda Bernard,* are also buried in the same vault.)

1819.—*John Owen Parr, Esq.* (*Elizabeth Mary,* his wife, is buried in the same vault.)

1820.—*William Nanson, Esq.*

1822.—*John Stephenson, Esq.* (*Mary,* his wife, is buried in the same vault.)

1823.—*Robert Raynsford, Esq.* Many years one of the stipendiary magistrates of the metropolis, and an active Vice-President of the Hospital. (*Elizabeth,* his wife, is buried in the same vault.)

1827.—*Philip Jackson, Esq.*

1830.—*John Heath, Esq.*† A justice of the peace for the county of Middlesex. (*Jane Louisa,* his wife, is buried in the same vault.)

1831.—*Thomas Smith, Esq.* (*Maria,* his wife, is buried in the same vault.)

1831.—*Richard Smith, Esq.* (*Elizabeth Ann,* his wife, is buried in the same vault.)

---

* Sir Thomas did not confine his charitable labours to the Foundling Hospital. He was indefatigable in forming Societies for bettering the condition of the poor, and in promoting the views of Charitable and Literary persons of all classes.

† Brother of the late Judge Heath, and father of John Benjamin Heath, Esq., His Sardinian Majesty's Consul General, and Governor of the Bank of England for the time being.

1832.—*The Right Honourable Lord Tenterden.* A Vice-President. The following inscription is placed under a marble bust of his lordship, in the eastern entrance to the Chapel:—

Prope . Situs . est
Carolus . Baro . Tenterden
Joannis . et . Aliciae . Abbott
filius . natu . minor
humillimae . sortis . parentibus
patre . vero . prudenti . matre . pia . ortus
scholae . regiae . Cantuariensis
postea . Collegii . Corporis . Christi . Oxon . alumnus
per . annos . xx . in . causis . versatus
primo . ad . communia . placita
mox . ad . placita . coram . ipso . rege . tenenda
Justiciarius
deinde . Justiciarius . Capitalis
gratia . demum . Georgii . IV . Regis
in . Baronum . ordinem . cooptatus
Quantum . apud . Britannos . honestus . labor
favente . deo . valeat
agnoscas . lector.

Haec . de . se . conscripsit
vir . summus . idemque . omnium . modestissimus
Vixit . annis . LXX
decessit . die . Nov . iv . anno . sacro . MDCCCXXXII
uxorem . duxit . Mariam
Joannis . Lagier . Lamotte . arm . filiam . natu maximam
quae . carissimo . marito
dies . non . amplius . XLV . superfuit
et . iuxta . sepulta . est
Parentibus . optimis . desideratissimis
liberi . moerentes
posuerunt

TRANSLATION.

Near . this . spot . lies
Charles . Baron . Tenterden
younger . son . of . John . and . Alice . Abbott.
Born . in . very . humble . station
of . a . Father . who . was . prudent
and . a . Mother . who . was . pious
He . was . brought . up . in . the . Grammar . School of . Canterbury
and . afterwards . at . Corpus . Christi . College . Oxford.
Having . practised . as . a . Barrister . for . twenty . years
He . became . Justice . of . the . Common . Pleas
was . removed . to . the . King's . Bench
there . raised . to . be . Chief . Justice
and . was . at . last . by . the . favour . of . King . George . IV.
created . a . Peer . of . the . Realm.
Learn . Reader
how . much . in . this . Country
may . under . the . blessing . of . God . be . attained
by . honest . industry.

The . above . is . the . notice . of . himself . left
by . one . of . the . most . eminent . as . well . as . most . modest . of . men.
He . died . aged . LXX . on . the . 4th . of . Nov. . MDCCCXXXII.
His . wife . Mary . eldest . daughter . of . John . Lagier . Lamotte . Esq.
survived . her . beloved . husband
only . xlv . days
and . is . buried . by . his . side.
This . Tablet . is . erected . to . the . memory
of . most . excellent . and . deeply . regretted . Parents
by . their . sorrowing . Children.*

---

* Lord Tenterden, before the labours of his judicial functions engrossed the whole of his time, took an active part in the administration of the affairs of the Foundling Hospital, and wrote the following verses, to be set to music, and sung at the commemorative festivals of the Governors :—

"The ship sail'd smoothly o'er the sea,
By gentle breezes fann'd,
When Coram, musing at the helm,
This happy fabric plann'd:
Not in the schools by sages taught
To woo fair virtue's form;
But nursed on danger's flinty lap,
And tutor'd by the storm.

1832.—*William Holden, Esq.*

1834.—*William Hammond, Esq.* (*Ann*, his wife, is buried in the same vault.)

1834.—*Christopher Stanger, M.D.* Thirty-seven years one of the Physicians to the Hospital.

1838.—*Charles James Johnstone, M.D.* The following is the inscription upon a monument erected in the eastern entrance of the Chapel, to the memory of this promising young Physician:—

"When threat'ning tempests round him rag'd,
And swelling billows heav'd,
His bark a wretched orphan seem'd,
Of aid and hope bereav'd.
If through the clouds a golden gleam
Broke sweetly from above,
He bless'd the smiling emblem there
Of charity and love.

"Around the glowing land he spread
Warm pity's magic spell,
And tender bosoms learn'd from him
With softer sighs to swell.
Beauty and wealth, and wit and power,
The various aid combin'd;
And angels smil'd upon the work
That Coram had design'd.

"Virtue and meekness mark'd his face
With characters benign,
And Hogarth's colours yet display
The lineaments divine:
Our ground his ashes sanctify,
Our songs his praise employs;
His spirit with the bless'd above
His full reward enjoys."

X

Carolo Jacobo Johnstone A. et M. B.
Coll. Cai. Gonv. Cantabr. Socio Hujus Hospitii alteri e Medicis
quem ægros assidue curantem Febri correptum mors occupavit
ante Diem VII. Kal. April. A. S. MDCCCXXXVIII. Æt. XXVIII :
viro pio probo comi Modesto
Egregie quum Medicinæ Tum Literarum Scienti
Amantissimo Suorum suis carissimo
Hunc Lapidem amici Ejus mœrentes
C. P. P. C.

TRANSLATION.

To
Charles James Johnstone,
Bachelor of Arts and of Medicine,
Fellow of Caius and Gonville College, Cambridge,
One of the two Physicians of this Hospital,
who was carried off
by fever caught in assiduous attention to the sick,
26th March, 1838,
in the twenty-eighth year of his age.
Pious, upright, amiable, unassuming;
eminently skilful as a Physician,
and no less distinguished as a Scholar;
most affectionate himself,
and most affectionately beloved.
This Tablet is erected by
His sorrowing friends.

1839.—*Arthur Browne Blakiston, Esq.*

1839.—*Samuel Compton Cox, Esq.* Thirty-three years Treasurer of the Hospital, and formerly one of the Masters of the High Court of Chancery. A monument has been erected, by the Governors, in the eastern entrance to the Chapel, to the memory of this excellent man, "*in gratitude for his Christian care of the objects of this Charity.*" (*Anna,** his wife, lies by his side in the same catacomb.)

* Daughter of the celebrated Percival Pott, Esq.—*Vide Nichols' Literary Anecdotes.*

1839.—*Sir Stephen Gaselee, Knight.* One of the Justices of the Court of Common Pleas, and a Vice-President of the Hospital. (*Lady Gaselee* is also buried in the same vault, together with *Henrietta* and *Emma*, their children.)

1839.—*Hugh Edwards, Esq.*

1840.—*Anthony V. D. Searle Van Dam, Esq.*

1842.—*Peregrine Dealtry, Esq.* Master of the Crown Office.

1844.—*The Rev. John Hewlett, B. D.* The following is the inscription on a very chaste mural monument, by Sievier, placed in the western entrance of the Chapel, in honour of this eminent Divine:—

In Memory of
The Reverend John Hewlett, B.D.
during XXIX Years Morning Preacher of this Hospital.
In style, he was forcible and clear;
in manner, grave and impressive;
Earnest in Exhortation
and sound in Doctrine;
his mind was richly stored
with ancient and modern Literature,
and his writings afford ample proofs
of scientific and theological attainments:
as a public reward for his Biblical labours,
The Earl of Liverpool, first Minister of the Crown,
presented him, in MDCCCXIX,
to the Rectory of Hilgay in Norfolk:
He discharged his various duties
throughout a long and useful life
with ability, diligence, and zeal,
attaching to himself in no ordinary degree
all with whom he was connected,
and died in Christian Faith and Hope
April 12th, MDCCCXLIV, aged LXXXVI.

ACADEMY OF MUSIC.

In July, 1774, Dr. Burney and Mr. Giardini, attended the Court of Governors, and proposed a plan for forming a *public music school* by means of the children of the Hospital, which, having been taken into consideration, was unanimously accepted as "likely to be of considerable advantage to this Corporation and of national utility."

The Court immediately set about opening a subscription roll (which received the support of the Dukes of Gloucester and Cumberland), and appointed a special Committee to "digest and form the properest method for carrying the said plan into execution," the Committee to consist of all the members of the Court present, and the Duke of Portland, the Earl of Ashburnham, the Earl of Dartmouth, Lord Le Despencer and Sir Watkin Williams Wynne, Bart.

But it was the fate of this scheme to be nipt in the bud. Its opponents proposed and carried a resolution at the next Court, which completely set it aside. The resolution was this—"It appeared to this Court that the plan of a public music school by way of employment of the children, is not warranted by the Act of Parliament."

Madame D'Arblay* in her Memoirs of Dr. Burney (her father), gives the following graphical account of this transaction:—

* The celebrated Miss Burney, author of "Evelina," &c.

"But neither the pain of his illness, nor the pleasure of his recovery, nor even the loved labours of his history, offered sufficient occupation for the insatiate activity of his mind. No sooner did he breathe again the breath of health, resume his daily business, and return to his nocturnal studies, than a project occurred to him of a new undertaking, which would have seemed to demand the whole time and undivided attention of almost any other man.

"This was nothing less than to establish, in England, a seminary for the education of musical pupils of both sexes, upon a plan of which the idea should be borrowed, though the execution should almost wholly be new modelled, from the Conservatorios of Naples and Vienna.

"As disappointment blighted this scheme, just as it seemed maturing to fruition, it would be to little purpose to enter minutely into its details; and yet, as it is a striking feature of the fervour of Dr. Burney for the advancement of his art, it is not its failure, through the secret workings of undermining prejudice, that ought to induce his biographer to omit recounting so interesting an intention and attempt; and the less, as a plan, in many respects similar, has recently been put into execution, without any reference to the original projector.

"The motives that suggested this undertaking to Dr. Burney, with the reasons by which they were influenced and supported, were to this effect—

"In England, where more splendid rewards await the favourite votaries of musical excellence than in any other spot on the globe, there was no establishment of any sort for forming such artists as might satisfy the real connoisseur in music; and save English talent from the mortification, and the British purse from the depredations of seeking a constant annual supply of genius and merit from foreign shores.

"An institution, therefore, of this character, seemed wanting to the state for national economy, and to the people for national encouragement.

"Such was the enlarged view which Dr. Burney, while yet in Italy, had taken of such a plan for his own country.

"The difficulty of collecting proper subjects to form its members, caused great diversity of opinion and of proposition amongst the advisers with whom Dr. Burney consulted.

"It was peculiarly necessary that these young disciples should be free from every sort of contamination, mental or corporal, upon entering this musical asylum, that they might spread no dangerous contagion of either sort, but be brought up to the practice of the art, with all its delightful powers of pleasing, chastened from their abuse.

"With such a perspective, to take promiscuously the children of the poor, merely where they had an ear for music, or a voice for song, would be running the risk of gathering together a mixed little multitude, which, from intermingling inherent vulgarity, hereditary diseases, or vicious propensities, with the finer qualities requisite for admission, might render the cultivation of their youthful talents a danger, if not a curse, to the country.

"Yet, the length of time that might be required for selecting little subjects of this unadulterated description from different quarters, with the next to impossibility of tracing, with any certainty, what might have been their real conduct in times past, or what might be their principles to give any basis of security for the time to come, caused a perplexity of the most serious species; for should a single one of the tribe go astray, the popular cry against teaching the arts to the poor would stamp the whole little community with a stain indelible, and the institution itself might be branded with infamy.

"What abstractedly was desirable, was, to try this experiment upon youthful beings to whom the world was utterly unknown, and who, not only in innocence had breathed their infantine lives, but in complete and unsuspicious ignorance of evil.

"Requisites so hard to obtain, and a dilemma so intricate to unravel, led the Doctor to think of the *Foundling Hospital,* in the neighbourhood of which, in Queen Square, stood his present dwelling.

"He communicated, therefore, his project to Sir Charles Whitworth, the Governor of the Hospital. Sir Charles thought it proper, feasible, desirable, and patriotic.

"The Doctor, thus seconded, drew up a plan for forming a musical conservatorio in the metropolis of England, and in the bosom of the *Foundling Hospital.*

"The intention was to collect from the whole little

corps all who had musical ears or tuneful voices, to be brought up scientifically as instrumental or vocal performers. Those of the group who gave no decided promise of such qualifications, were to go on with their ordinary education, and to abide by its ordinary result, according to the original regulations of the charity.

"A meeting of the Governors and Directors was convened by their chief, Sir Charles Whitworth, for announcing this scheme. The plan was heard with general approbation, but the discussions to which it gave rise were discursive and perplexing.

"It was objected, that music was an art of luxury, by no means requisite to life, or accessary to morality. These children were all meant to be educated as plain but essential members of the general community. They were to be trained up to useful purposes, with a singleness that would ward off all ambition for what was higher, and teach them to repay the benefit of their support by cheerful labour. To stimulate them to superior views might mar the religious object of the charity, which was to nullify, rather than extinguish, all disposition to pride, vice, or voluptuousness, such as, probably, had demoralized their culpable parents, and thrown these deserted outcasts upon the mercy of the *Foundling Hospital.*

"This representation, the Doctor acknowledged, would be unanswerable, if it were decided to be right, and if it were judged to be possible, wholly to extirpate the art of music in the British empire, or, if the *Foundling Hospital* were to be considered as a seminary, predestined to menial servitude, and as the only institution of the country where the members were to form a caste, from whose rules and plodden ways no genius could ever emerge.

"But such a fiat could never be issued by John Bull, nor so flat a stamp be struck upon any portion of his countrymen. John Bull was at once too liberal and too proud to seek to adopt the tame ordinances of the immutable Hindoos, with whom ages passed unmarked, generations unchanged, the poor never richer, the simple never wiser, and with whom, family by family, and trade by trade, begin, continue, and terminate their monotonous existence by the same predetermined course, and to the same invariable destiny.

"These children, the Doctor answered, are all orphans; they are taken from no family, for by none are they owned: they are drawn from no calling, for to none are they specifically bred. They are all brought up to menial offices, though they are all instructed in reading and writing, and the females in needle-work; but they are all, systematically and indiscriminately, destined to be servants or apprentices at the age of fifteen; from which period, all their hold upon the benevolent institution to which they are indebted for their infantine rescue from perishing cold and starving want, with their subsequent maintenance and tuition, is rotatorily transferred to new-born claimants; for the Hospital then has fulfilled its engagements, and the children must go forth to the world, whether to their benefit or their disgrace.

"Were it not better, then, when there are subjects who are success-inviting, to bestow upon them professional improvement, with virtuous education? since, as long as operas, concerts, and theatres are licensed by government, musical performers, vocal and instrumental, will inevitably be wanted, employed, and remunerated: and every state is surely best served, and the people of every country are surely the most encouraged, when the nation suffices for itself, and no foreign aid is necessarily called in, to share either the fame or the emoluments of public performances.

"Stop, then; prohibit, proscribe—if it be possible—all taste for foreign refinements, and for the exquisite finishing of foreign melody and harmony, or establish a school on our own soil, in which, as in painting and in sculpture, the foreign perfection of arts may be taught, transplanted, and culled, till they become indigenous.

"And where, if not here, may subjects be found on whom such a national trial may be made with the least danger of injury? Subjects who have been brought up with a strictness of regular habits that has warded them from all previous mischief, yet who are too helpless and ignorant, as well as poor, to be able to develop whether or not nature, in her secret workings, has kindled within their unconscious bosoms a spark—a single spark of harmonic fire, that might light them from being hewers of wood and brushers of spiders, to those regions of vocal and instrumental excellence, that might propitiate the project of drawing from our own culture a school for music, of which the students, under proper moral and religious tutelage, might, in time, supersede the foreign auxiliaries by whom they are now utterly extinguished.

"The objectors were charged, also, to weigh well that there was no law or regulation, and no means whatsoever that could prevent any of this little association from becoming singers and players, if they had musical powers, and such should be their wish; though, if self-thrown into that walk, singers and players only at the lowest theatres, or at the tea and public gardens, or even in the streets, as fiddlers of country dances, or as ballad squallers, in which degraded exercise of their untaught endowments, not only decent life must necessarily be abandoned, but immorality, licentiousness, and riot, must assimilate with, or rather form a prominent part of their exhibitions and performances.

"Here the discussion closed. The opponents were silenced, if not convinced, and the trial of the project was decreed. The hardly-fought battle over, victory, waving her gay banners, that wafted to the Doctor hopes of future renown with present benediction, determined him, for the moment, to relinquish even his history, that he might devote every voluntary thought to consolidating this scheme.

"The primary object of his consideration, because the most conscientious, was the preservation of the morals and fair conduct of the pupils. And here, the exemplary character and the purity of the principles of Dr. Burney, would have shone forth to national advantage, had the expected prosperity of his design brought his meditated regulations into practice.

"Vain would it be to attempt, and useless, if not vain, to describe his indignant consternation, when, while in the full occupation of these arrangements, a letter arrived to him from Sir Charles Whitworth, to make known, with great regret, that the undertaking was suddenly overthrown. The enemies to the attempt, who had seemed quashed, had merely lurked in ambush, to watch for an unsuspected moment to convene a partial committee, in which they voted out the scheme as an innovation upon the original purpose of the institution; and pleading, also, an old act of Parliament against its adoption, they solemnly proscribed it for ever.*

"Yet a repeal of that act had been fully intended, before the plan, which, hitherto, had only been agitating and negotiating, should have been put into execution.

"All of choice, however, and all of respect that

* This apparent want of liberality on the part of the Governors, in the mental culture of the children, reminds one of a darker period of the history of this small community. Dr. Johnson writes, in 1756:—"When, a few months ago, I wandered through the Hospital, I found not a child that seemed to have heard of his creed or the commandments. To breed up children in this manner, is to rescue them from an early grave, that they may find employment for the gibbet: from dying in innocence, that they may perish by their crimes."

remained for Dr. Burney, consisted in a personal offer from Sir Charles Whitworth, to re-assemble an opposing meeting amongst those friends who, previously, had carried the day.

"But happy as the Doctor would have been to have gained, with the honour of general approbation, a point he had elaborately studied to clear from mystifying objections, and to render desirable even to patriotism, his pride was justly hurt by so abrupt a defalcation; and he would neither with open hostility, nor under any versatile contest, become the founder or chief of so important an enterprise.

"He gave up, therefore, the attempt, without further struggle; simply recommending to the mature reflections of the members of the last Committee, whether it were not more pious, as well as more rational, to endeavour to ameliorate the character and lives of practical musical noviciates, than to behold the nation, in its highest classes, cherish the art, follow it, embellish it with riches, and make it fashion and pleasure, while, to train to that art, with whatever precautions, its appropriate votaries from the bosom of our own country, seemed to call for opposition, and to deserve condemnation.

"Thus died, in its birth, this interesting project, which, but for this brief sketch, might never have been known to have brightened the mind, as one of the projects, or to have mortified it, as one of the failures, of the active and useful life of Dr. Burney."

ADMISSION OF CHILDREN.

The first admission of Children took place in 1741, under the following advertisement :—

" To-morrow, at eight o'clock in the evening, this house will be opened for the reception of twenty children, under the following regulations :—

" No child exceeding the age of two months will be taken in, nor such as have the evil, leprosy, or disease of the like nature, whereby the health of the other children may be endangered ; for the discovery whereof, every child is to be inspected as soon as it is brought, and the person who brings it is to come in at the outward door and ring a bell at the inward door, and not to go away until the child is returned or notice given of its reception ; but no questions whatever will be asked of any person who brings a child, nor shall any servant of the house presume to endeavour to discover who such person is, on pain of being discharged.

" All persons who bring children are requested to affix on each child some particular writing, or other distinguishing mark or token, so that the children may be known hereafter if necessary."

These receptions of children took place occasionally in the same manner, and were necessarily regulated by the funds of the Hospital, which being derived from private subscriptions and legacies of benevolent individuals only, were of course limited.

As the Hospital became more generally known, it will readily be supposed that the applications for admission greatly increased, so that there were frequently one hundred women at the door when twenty children only could be received. This gave rise to the disgraceful scene of women scrambling and fighting to get to the door, that they might be of the fortunate few to reap the benefit of the Asylum.

To obviate this evil a new method was adopted, by which all women bringing children were admitted into the court-room, and there sat on benches, with strict orders not to stir from their seats. Then, as many white balls as there were children to be taken in, with five red balls for every twenty children to be received, and so in proportion for any greater or less number; and as many black balls, as with the white and red, were equal to the number of women present, were put into a bag or box, which was handed round to the women; each woman who drew a white ball was sent, with her child, to the inspecting-room, that it might undergo the usual examination. Every woman who drew a black ball was immediately turned out of the house with her infant; and every woman who drew a red ball was taken, with her child, into another room, there to remain until the examination of the children for whom white balls were drawn was ended, and if, on such examination, any of those children were rejected, for reasons stated in the public notice, ballots were taken, after a similar manner, for filling up the vacancies, till the whole number was completed. This plan, it is true, prevented the disgraceful scenes described; but a charity so unguardedly dispensed, as to the selection of its objects, could not but open the door to fraud and abuse of the worst description. We know that no human institution, however cautiously managed, can be *wholly* free from abuse; some daring Clodius will always be found to pollute the mysteries, let the house be ever so carefully watched. If this be true in ordinary cases, surely it must have required more than common caution in setting on foot an asylum, the opening of which, if not carefully effected, would let loose as many evils as ever issued from Pandora's box. This was evidently felt by Captain Coram himself, who, in the memorial which he presented to George the Second, as a recommendation of his design, throws out the cautionary suggestion,—that its success could only be insured, "*provided due and proper care be taken for setting on foot so necessary an establishment.*" He no sooner found, therefore, that the managers were acting upon a principle which furnished no guarantee for the effectual operation of the charity, namely—receiving children without establishing any test by which the merits of each case could be ascertained, than he opposed their proceedings; but after repeated admonition, finding his advice disregarded by the majority of the Committee, he left the management of the institution altogether in their hands.*

* Of the particular cause of disagreement between Captain Coram and the managing Committee there is no record. The following extract from the will of Anthony Allen, Esq., dated 1753, shows, however, that the Founder was supported in his objections to their proceedings by one, at least, of his friends :—

"And whereas, many years before the obtaining the royal charter for the

The system above referred to continued for a period of fifteen years, viz.—from 1741 to 1756, during which, 1384 children were received, or, upon an average, ninety-two annually.

The managers, however, looked forward all along to the time when they should be able to open their Hospital upon the most unrestricted plan, and many were the abortive schemes suggested for the acquirement of wealth to enable them to do so; but it was obvious, that no power or means, except Parliamentary, could be devised for effectually meeting the object. To Parliament, therefore, the Governors appealed, having previously ascertained that George the Second had a good feeling towards their design. The following resolutions of the House of Commons, of the 6th April, 1756, sufficiently prove the success with which the application was attended:—

"That the enabling the Hospital for the maintenance and education of exposed and deserted young children to receive all the children that shall be

---

Hospital for exposed and deserted young children, I did, at the instance of that indefatigable schemist, Captain Thomas Coram, really intend some considerable benefaction towards carrying on so good a project, and did encourage the concurrence of other liberal benefactors, till some of the acting Governors and Guardians of the said Hospital went counter to our judgments and proposal pressed upon them by the said Coram, on several occasions, which made me withhold my hand, saving the sum of sixteen guineas I advanced as necessity urged, from time to time, towards the immediate subsistence of the said Mr. Coram, who had exhausted his whole substance in soliciting that charter during about seventeen years, never meeting any relief from the said Hospital, I now will that £200, besides the said £16 16*s.* so paid, be given to the use of the said Hospital, within two years after my decease, in lieu of all claims and pretensions the said Hospital may make on that score."

offered, is the only method to render that charitable institution of lasting and general utility.

"That to render the said Hospital of lasting and general utility, the assistance of Parliament is necessary.

"That to render the said Hospital of general utility and effect, it should be enabled to appoint proper places in all counties, ridings, or divisions of this kingdom, for the reception of all exposed and deserted young children."

Added to these resolutions, a guarantee was given by Parliament that it would provide the means, by liberal grants of money, to enable the Governors to carry out this extensive scheme of charity.

A basket was accordingly hung outside of the gates of the Hospital, and an advertisement publicly announced, that all children under the age of two months, tendered for admission, would be received.

In pursuance of which, on the 2nd June, 1756, being the first day of general reception, 117 children were given up to the fostering care of the state!

Though the Governors of the charity, in anticipation of parochial interference, had armed themselves with the special power of the law for their protection, yet they discovered that no authority, however great, could prevent parish officers from emptying their workhouses of the infant poor, and transferring them to this general sanctuary provided by government. Had they stopped here, the morality of their conduct would not, perhaps, have been questioned; but it was the frequent practice of these daring authorities, sometimes in conjunction with the brutal father, to rob the poor mother of her new-born infant, whilst she was in a state of helplessness from the effects of her recent confinement, and to convey it to the Hospital, that they might be rid of the burden of maintaining it. The scenes which daily occurred at the asylum from this circumstance, would have moved the stoutest heart.

The managers did all they could to prevent this infamous practice, by prosecuting the delinquents, but the motive was too strong to be put down; it continued in spite of their efforts.

When a Foundling Hospital was established in Paris, in the year 1640, its objects were limited to the children found exposed in that city, and its suburbs; and it was understood by those who furthered a similar design in this country, that its operation would, in the same manner, be confined to London and its environs. But benefits so tempting being irresistable to persons in country towns, they were determined to share with the good people of London, a privilege which they considered common to all. "There is set up in our Corporation" (writes a correspondent from a town three hundred miles distant, in one of the chronicles of the day), "a new and uncommon trade, namely, the conveying children to the Foundling Hospital. The person employed in this trade is a woman of notoriously bad character. She undertakes the carrying of these children at so much per head. She has, I am told, made one trip already; and is now set upon her journey with two of her daughters, each with a child on her back." The writer then very properly suggests, that it ought to be ascertained "whether or not these poor infants do really arrive at their destination, or what becomes of them." That such an inquiry was necessary, there is no doubt;—the sequel will prove it.

At Monmouth, a person was tried for the murder of his child, which was found drowned with a stone about its neck! when the prisoner proved that he delivered it to a travelling tinker, who received a guinea from him to carry it to the Hospital. Nay, it was publicly asserted in the House of Commons, that one man who had the charge of five infants in baskets, happened in his journey to get intoxicated, and lay all night asleep on a common; and in the morning he found three of the five children he had in charge actually dead! Also, that of eight infants brought out of the country at one time in a waggon, seven died before it reached London: the surviving child owing its life to the solicitude of its mother; who rather than commit it alone to the carrier, followed the waggon on foot, occasionally affording her infant the nourishment it required.

It was further stated, that a man on horseback, going to London with luggage in two panniers, was overtaken at Highgate, and being asked what he had in his panniers, answered, "I have two children in each: I brought them from Yorkshire for the Foundling Hospital, and used to have eight guineas a trip; but lately another man has set up against me, which has lowered my price."

This practice of transporting children from remote towns was condemned by a distinct resolution of the House of Commons, and a Bill was ordered to be brought in to prevent it; but this Bill was never presented, so that parish officers and others still continued to carry on their illicit trade, by delivering children to vagrants, who, for a small sum of money, undertook the task of conveying them to the Hospital, although they were in no condition to take care of them, whereby numbers perished for want, or were otherwise destroyed; and even in cases where children were really left at the Hospital, the barbarous wretches who had the conveying of them, not content with the gratuity they received, stript the poor infants of their clothing into the bargain, leaving them naked in the basket at the Hospital gate.*

A system so void of all order and discretion, must necessarily have occasioned many difficulties: for instance, it frequently happened, that persons who sent their children to the Hospital, having nothing to prove their reception, were suspected, or, if not suspected, were charged by their malevolent neighbours with destroying them, and were consequently cited before a magistrate of the district to shew to the contrary. This they could only do by procuring an examination of the Hospital registers; and the

* The following is a strong instance of the vicissitudes of life:—A few years since, an aged Banker in the north of England, received into the Hospital at the above period, was desirous of becoming acquainted with his origin, when, all the information afforded by the books of the establishment was, that he was put into the basket at the gate *naked*.

Governors were frequently called upon for certificates of the fact, before the party could be released. This inconvenience was, however, afterwards obviated, by the practice of giving a billet to each person who brought a child, acknowledging its reception.

But the difficulty which presented itself paramount to all others, related to the manner in which so great a number of children was to be reared. In the first year of this indiscriminate admission, the number received was 3,296; in the second year, 4,085; in the third, 4,229; and during less than ten months of the fourth year (after which the system of indiscriminate reception was abolished), 3,324. Thus, in this short period, no less than 14,934 infants were cast on the compassionate protection of the public! It necessarily became a question how the lives of this army of infants could be best preserved; and the Governors, not being able to settle this point among themselves, addressed certain queries to the College of Physicians, which were promptly answered, by recommending a course of treatment consonant to nature and common sense! Children, deprived as these were of their natural aliment, required more than usual watchfulness; and although, on a small scale, the providing a given number of healthy wet-nurses, as substitutes for the mothers of infants, would have been an easy task, yet, when they arrived in numbers so considerable, the Governors found that the object they had in view must necessarily fail from its very magnitude.

It has been truly said, that the frail tenure by

which an infant holds its life, will not allow of a remitted attention even for a few hours: who, therefore, will be surprised, after hearing under what circumstances most of these poor children were left at the Hospital gate, that, instead of being a protection to the living, the institution became, as it were, a charnel-house for the dead! It is a notorious fact, that many of the infants received at the gate, did not live to be carried into the wards of the building; and from the impossibility of procuring a sufficient number of proper nurses, the emaciated and diseased state in which many of these children were brought to the Hospital, and the malconduct of some of those to whose care they were committed (notwithstanding these nurses were under the superintendence of certain ladies—sisters of charity), the deaths amongst them were so frequent, that of the 14,934 received, only 4,400 lived to be apprenticed out, being a mortality of more than seventy per cent!* Thus was the institution (conducted on a plan so wild and chimerical, and so widely differing

* These details are appalling enough; but the account given of the Dublin Foundling Hospital, at a later period, greatly surpasses them:—"Of 12,641 children received in six years, ending the 24th of June, 1796, so many as 9,804 had died; 2,692 were unaccounted for, and only 145 were to be traced. In the infirmary the mortality had been still more shocking. Of 5,216 children sent into the infirmary in those six years, three individuals only came out of the walls alive. These facts were ascertained on the oaths of the culprits themselves, and were occasioned partly by gross negligence, and partly by the radical defect of the system of a general admission of this nature, which has a direct and uncontrollable tendency to encourage the vice, and increase the mortality of our species."—*Life of Sir Thomas Bernard, Bart., by Rev. James Baker.*

from its original design), found to be diseased in its very vitals. The avowed object of saving life was frustrated by a variety of contingent circumstances; and the permanent and two-fold benefit of which it was intended to have been the instrument, under the regulations contemplated by the Founder, was set aside by a system of fraud and abuse, which entailed on the public an immense annual expenditure,* without even *one* good result. To establish a market for *vice* to carry on her profligate trade without let or hindrance; to arrest the first step towards repentance of one yet in the infancy of crime, by pointing out the way in which she might perpetuate her guilt with impunity; to break the beautiful chain of the affections which characterizes mankind as social beings, by giving a general license to parents to desert their offspring, upon the barbarous plea that they cannot easily maintain them; to wink as it were, at fraud, by showing how designing persons might dispose of children entrusted to their guardianship, and prevent a discovery of their guilty acts: these were some of the evils which were re-

* The total expense was about £500,000! Several propositions were made, ridding the country of the burthen, and amongst them the following:—"His Majesty having recommended the case of the Foundling Hospital to the House of Commons, which cheerfully granted £40,000 for the support of that charity, the growing annual expense of it appeared worthy of further consideration, and leave was granted to bring in a bill for obliging all the parishes of England and Wales to keep registers of all their deaths, births, and marriages, that from these a fund might be raised towards the support of the said Hospital. The bill was accordingly prepared by a committee appointed for the purpose, but before the House could take the report into consideration, the Parliament was prorogued."—*Smollett.*

alized in the early proceedings of the Governors, for want of attention to the cautionary suggestion of the Founder, to " take due and proper care in setting on foot so necessary an establishment."

But the state of things described could not possibly last long, except in a community lost to all decency and order. No sooner, therefore, did those who had promoted a system fraught with so much mischief, discover the error they had committed, than they wished to retrace their steps :—the moralist enlisted his pen in a cause which he found was endangered by its continuance; and mercy stepped forward to arrest the destroying hand of death, to whose vengeance so many infants had been doomed, under the sanction of this unwise administration of the charity: and at length, Parliament, which by its inadvertence had promoted the evil, annulled its sanction thereto, by declaring—*That the indiscriminate admission of all children under a certain age into the Hospital, had been attended with many evil consequences, and that it be discontinued.*

After the House of Commons had passed the resolution which annulled the practice of receiving children in such an unguarded and indiscriminate manner, the Governors were left to adopt what they conceived to be the views of the Founder, and to place the institution upon that basis of prudential charity on which it now stands.

Tokens.—It will be seen, that one of the regulations at the outset was, that persons leaving children should "affix on them some particular writing, or other distinguishing mark or token." Forty years ago, the Governors being curiously inclined, appointed a committee to inspect these tokens, with the view of ascertaining their general nature, which committee, having examined a portion of them, reported the following to be specimens of the whole: viz.—

A half-crown, of the reign of Queen Anne, with hair.

An old silk purse.

A silver fourpence and an ivory fish.

A stone cross, set in silver.

A shilling, of the reign of James the Second.

A silver fourpence of William and Mary, and a silver penny of King James.

A silver fourpence.

A small gold locket.

A silver coin (foreign), of sixpence value.

In 1757, a lottery ticket was given in with a child, but whether it turned up a prize or a blank is not recorded.

The following lines were pinned to the clothes of one of the deserted infants:—

> "Go, gentle babe, thy future life be spent
> In virtuous purity and calm content;
> Life's sunshine bless thee, and no anxious care
> Sit on thy brow, and draw the falling tear;
> Thy country's grateful servant may'st thou prove,
> And all thy life be happiness and love."

Another child, received on the first day of admission, had the following doggrel lines affixed to its clothes:—

> " Pray use me well, and you shall find
> My father will not prove unkind
> Unto that nurse who's my protector,
> Because he is a benefactor."

At this period, the station in life of the parties availing themselves of the charity, could only be surmised by the quality of the garments in which the children were dressed, the particulars of which were faithfully recorded; the following being a sample, viz.—

" 1741.—A male child, about two months old, with white dimity sleeves, lined with white, and tied with red ribbon."

" A female child, aged about six weeks, with a blue figured ribbon, and purple and white printed linen sleeves, turned up with red and white."

" A male child, about a fortnight old, very neatly dressed; a fine holland cap, with a cambric border, white corded dimity sleeves, the shirt ruffled with cambric."

" A male child, a week old; a holland cap, with a plain border, edged biggin and forehead-cloth, diaper bib, striped and flowered dimity mantle, and another holland one; India dimity sleeves, turned up with stitched holland, damask waistcoat, holland ruffled shirt." *

* The compiler hopes to be pardoned for introducing here a nursery

Sometimes the recording clerk was rather laconic

scene, from a little work published by him some years ago, illustrative of this portion of our history:—

"The infant having been examined, and deemed admissible, was forwarded to the charge of the nurses, in the long room, up stairs; a particular account being first taken of each article of clothing, token, or writing left with it.

"'I 'faith, here's a bonny babe,' said nurse Simkins, as she received it from one of the women below; 'and well bedizened too,' continued she; 'what with its laced cap and Indie frock, and the like.'

'Ay, ay,' cried the shrill voice of nurse Thompson, 'folk don't come here veiled for nothing.'

'Hush!' replied the cautious Simkins; 'don't you know it's against orders to look at the women folk who bring their children?'

'Never mind, never mind,' said nurse Thompson, 'they can't hang a body for peeping.'

'No, nor for speaking neither,' whispered nurse Dormouse.

'Gimini!' exclaimed nurse Simkins, as she examined the infant; 'of all the things in the world, here's a picture round the neck of the babe!'

"Upon this exclamation the worthies of the nursery congregated about nurse Simkins and the infant.

'I'll bet my Sunday cap,' said nurse Thompson, 'there's been foul play with this pretty babe: look at the fair face of the lady in the picture, and swear, if ye can, she's not its mother.'

'Ay—you're right,' whispered nurse Dormouse.

'Well, well,' cried old nurse Mathews, for the first time opening her mouth, 'good looks buy nothing in the market, as the saying is: things are strangely altered since *I* was a young woman. What would the girls in *my* day have given for such opportunities of getting rid of their bairns? There was poor Nancy Martin for instance, who was with bairn by that young rogue, Tom Hodges, the sexton's son, who said he would wed her, and all that, and then went over the seas, never to return. Well, as I was a saying, the parish folk made her to stand in the church for three Sundays, in a white sheet, to do penance as they calls it. One thing is certain—they broke her heart, and so she died. Well, well, crosses are but ladders that do lead up to heaven, as the saying is.'

'Between ourselves,' said nurse Dormouse, venturing to raise her voice one note above a whisper, 'I think the wise ones here are marvellously gull'd: what is to prevent King George himself from sending his base-born?'

'Ay, ay—very true, very true,' cried the nursery coterie with unanimous voice, winking at each other to mark the sagacity of the observation.

and quaint in his descriptions: for instance, of one of the children he says, it had

"A paper on the breast—
Clout over the head."

There is so great a misapprehension* in the public mind regarding the present objects and purposes of the Foundling Hospital, that it is necessary to enter

'I say nothing,' cried nurse Mathews; 'but if all fools wore white caps, we should look very like a flock of geese, though, for all that.'

"This piece of wit drew from the gossips a hearty laugh, which, however, was suddenly stopped by a cry of 'hark!' from the cautious nurse Simkins; ''tis the matron's step,' said she; and with one accord they dispersed about the room, and were as busy in their vocation as ever—in the performance of which the reader, perhaps, has no desire again to disturb them."—*Hans Sloane, a Tale.*

* This misapprehension is perpetuated, no doubt, by the Governors retaining a title to their Hospital not strictly warranted by its present objects or practice; and it may be questionable whether the interests of the charity are advanced by their doing so. Such cognomen is not called for by any enactment either in the charter or act of Parliament. The following is a criticism of Lord Brougham on this subject:—

"Machiavel says, that, in political affairs, you should beware lest, in changing the name, you alter the thing, without intending it: but he also says, that it is sometimes good, when you should change the thing, to keep the name. This maxim has been fully acted upon in the case of the London Foundling Hospital, and I have seen the bad consequence of following the Machiavelian rule. When lately in France, I made war on Foundling Hospitals, and I found a formidable host of prejudices embodied in their defence—a host the more dangerous, that they had been enlisted in the service by the purest feelings of benevolence; those persons I found citing against me the supposed fact, that we have, in this metropolis, a Foundling Hospital—indeed, a street, deriving its name from thence, and a quarter of the town its property. My simple answer was, that the name alone has been for half a century known amongst us, the thing itself having long since been put down with consent of Parliament."—*Vide his Lordship's speech in the House of Lords*, 21*st May*, 1835.

At the back of an original draft for a charter for the Hospital, it is called "The Orphanotrophy," or nursery for orphans.

into this important branch of the charity with some particularity; and first, it will be well to revert to the views of the Founder, and to the proceedings of the early managers of the institution.

The Intentions of the Founder.—It has been before related, that when Captain Coram resided at Rotherhithe, about the year 1720, his avocations obliging him to go early into the city, and return late, he frequently saw infants exposed and deserted in the public streets; and as there was but one step in his active mind from the knowledge of an evil to a desire for remedying it, he immediately set about inquiring into the probable causes for so outrageous a departure from humanity and natural affection.

He knew, what every man who studies the human heart must know—that the motive to such a dereliction of maternal duty must be beyond the ordinary casualties of indigence. He was not long in discovering the true source of the evil. He found that it arose out of a morbid morality, then possessing the public mind, by which an unhappy female, who fell a victim to the seductions and false promises of designing men, was left to hopeless contumely, and irretrievable disgrace. Neither she nor the offspring of her guilt appear to have been admitted within the pale of human compassion: her first false step was her final doom, without even the chance, however desirous, of returning to the road of rectitude. All the consideration which was given to her condition, was the enactment of laws to bring her to *punishment*, after she had been driven to the commission of the worst of crimes: for the error of a day, she was punished with the infamy of years; and although her departure from the path of virtue, so far from being the consequence of a previous vicious disposition, might have been brought about by an artful scheme of treachery, she was branded for ever as a woman habitually lewd. These evils necessarily increased the quantum of crime in society, according to the manner in which they operated upon the unfortunate individuals under their influence;—still no one stepped forward to provide a remedy. The legislature, from time to time, condemned the unhappy wretch to capital punishment who should, in the madness of despair, lift her arm against the child of her guilt; but it never once considered the means by which both parent and child might be saved from destruction: yet, by a strange perversity, those very laws bore on the face of them evidence of the necessity and justice of some more Christian proceeding. In all of them, the crime for which the punishment was awarded, is stated to have been committed from a desire in the mother to "*avoid her shame.*" Surely the woman who would make so great a struggle to preserve her reputation, as to break the natural ties which bind parent to offspring, who is willing to forego the endearments which are the fruits of her situation, by either sacrificing or deserting her child, cannot, with justice, be charged as habitually lewd!—a lewd woman has no shame to hide—she makes a show of her guilt, and claims, in open day, the protection which she knows has been provided for her by the poor-laws. But when a woman, with a sense of honour, finds herself the unsuspecting victim of treachery, with the witness of her disgrace hanging about her neck, in the person of her child, left to the reproach of the world and her own conscience, and seeing no other means of saving her character, she becomes delirious in her despair, and vents her fury on the consequences of her seduction—the child of her seducer! Hence the murder and desertion of children became alarming evils—evils which were produced and perpetuated "*for want*" (to use the words of Captain Coram) "*of proper means for preventing the disgrace and succouring the necessities of their parents.*" He therefore proposed to erect a sanctuary, to which these wretched mothers might fly, and there deposit the offspring and the secret of an unhallowed intercourse, and be thus enabled to return to that path from which they had unguardedly strayed.

This was doubtless the object of Captain Coram. In all his memorials to persons of distinction, soliciting their support, he ascribes to the parent, as the motive of her cruel conduct towards her offspring, a desire to preserve her reputation,—to "*hide her shame;*" and in Hogarth's design, illustrating the views of the Founder, it will be seen that he makes him hold personal communion with the penitential mother, pouring into her heart the oil of gladness, whilst he relieves her of the child of her sorrow. To accomplish his purpose of founding an hospital for the objects described, Captain Coram with his usual zeal endeavoured to enlist the sympathies of the humane and charitable. He soon found, however, that there were obstacles in the way. They who admitted the evil, questioned the remedy, and doubted whether it might not prove greater than the disease. He was for seventeen years combating public opinion on this head, and though he at last prevailed, it was after many contests between himself and others as to the probable issue. Can it be wondered at, therefore, that in addressing the President at the first meeting of the Governors after the charter had been granted, he should throw out a suggestion, that its success could only be secured "*provided due and proper care be taken for setting on foot so necessary an establishment.*" This, besides being dictated by his own good sense, was also forced upon him by those who aided him in his scheme, and was the condition upon which they gave him their support. This "due and proper care" could only refer to the selection of the objects, and it has been seen in preceding pages with what absence of forethought the Hospital was "set on foot," and the evil consequences which arose therefrom.

At the very outset an error was committed. Captain Coram, and those who assisted him, petitioned for two objects:—first, "to *prevent* the frequent murders of poor miserable infants at their birth;" secondly, "to *suppress* the inhuman custom of exposing new-born infants to perish in the streets."

Now to accomplish these objects, the Charter incorporated an "Hospital for the maintenance and education of *exposed* and *deserted* young children," thus giving a licence to that which was contrary to law, and which the memorialists were desirous to *suppress.* It was clear, therefore, that such a charter, though beneficial as regards the rights and privileges which it gave to the Governors, as a corporation, was useless as respected the main object, namely, the admission of children,—and so it proved. In the next session of Parliament, after the charter was granted, the Governors found it necessary to frame a bill to *explain* and enlarge the powers granted to them. This bill passed into a law ; and the preamble affords the explanation required, by stating that the Hospital is for infants who are *liable* to be exposed in the streets, or to be murdered by their parents. Now there are two causes which may suggest themselves to the reader, as likely to lead to the exposition or destruction of infants : namely, *inability of parents to maintain them,* or a *wanton inhumanity.* With respect to the first,—though this miserable plea has been sanctioned in countries where humanity and morality have made but little progress, yet in England it is altogether without foundation, for the wise and systematic provision which has been made for the relief of *indigence,* by the institution of poor-laws, takes from poverty the desperate alternative to which it might otherwise be exposed. As to the second cause,—*wanton inhumanity,* it may be said, that however the barbarous policy of eastern countries may render callous the human heart to the calls of parental affection,—in this country, where the mild influences of Christianity strengthen and support the natural ties which bind parent to offspring, the wanton sacrifice of infant life is happily of rare occurrence. It will then be asked, "*what* children are *liable* to be exposed and destroyed by their parents?" It is answered,—the children of those wretched mothers, before described, whose combination of mental and bodily distress admits of no *partial* relief,—no relief which the poor-laws can effectually bestow. These were the objects which fell under the compassionate consideration of Captain Coram, and the non-attention of the early Governors to his cautionary suggestion, produced the lamentable consequences already narrated, and caused the Founder himself to secede from the Council Board of the Institution.

Children received with Money.—After Parliament (frightened by the spirit of evil itself had raised) had deserted the Charity, the Governors were left to pursue, once more, their own course, and to adapt, if they thought fit, its administration to the more immediate objects of the Founder. This they were evidently desirous of doing, but the extravagancies caused by the "nationality" of their Institution for the period alluded to, had emptied the exchequer of the Hospital, and the evils of the system had so offended the public, that much of the individual support which it previously received from charitable persons was withdrawn.

Their "poverty," perhaps not the "will" of the acting Governors, led them into an error of another kind, namely—a resolution to receive children with *money*, in addition to such other objects as the funds of the Hospital might enable them to maintain. It is a fact, much to be regretted, that for many years children were mysteriously received on payment of £100, without a knowledge of, or any clue being given to the parents from whom they sprung! The abuses which might, and no doubt did arise from this system, are so obvious as to need no comment.* It

* That such a practice should be attended by much of the romance of real life will readily be supposed. For instance, it is related, that a married woman, whose husband was in India, whilst she was on a visit to England with some friends, had formed an improper *liason* with a gentleman, which resulted in her finding herself in a situation, which, under other circumstances, would have been called *interesting*. That in this dilemma, her husband being expected home at no distant period, and the fact of her situation being unknown to her friends, she consulted an eminent physician, who, ingenious in expedients, asked her if she was prepared to bear pain heroically and to follow his instructions, to which she replied in the affirmative. That he then caused her to be confined to her bed under an assumed illness, and having introduced a nurse into the house who was in the secret, she was delivered of a child, without any of her friends being aware of what had happened to her; the child having been, at the instant of its birth, conveyed secretly out of the house of her friend, and sent to the Foundling Hospital, with the necessary sum of money, without any questions being asked on either side.

About the same period of time the following case occurred. A daughter of a general in the army, of a distinguished family (a girl seventeen years old), formed, in the most unaccountable manner, an illicit *liason* with a menial servant in her father's house. On the discovery of the melancholy circumstance, the enraged parent, after committing upon his delinquent daughter personal violence, which nothing but temporary insanity could have prompted, turned her out of doors, and, as far as he was concerned, would have left her to starve in the streets. After this, he gave out to his friends that she was dead, and the whole family went into mourning for her loss. She was delivered of a child, which was placed

is due, however, to the Governors to say, that immediately after the funds of the charity had assumed a healthier state, they abolished altogether this more than questionable practice. At a Court of Governors, held on the 21st January, 1801, there being present several eminent lawyers, including Mr. (afterwards Baron) Garrow, and Sir Thomas Plumer (subsequently Master of the Rolls), it was resolved to rescind the obnoxious bye-law which originated so objectionable a system. The truth is, the matter was about to be brought to a legal issue, from the following circumstance:—The mother of a child which had been received under this rule, although a consenting party to the separation, afterwards repented and having discovered the residence of the nurse with whom it was placed in the country, practiced upon her an artifice by which she obtained possession of the child and refused to relinquish her right. The Governors feeling themselves under an obligation to reclaim the child by exercising the powers which they conceived to be vested in them,

---

in the Foundling Hospital. Subsequently to this event, the father of the wretched mother so far relented, as to cause her to be placed with a milliner in a distant county, upon condition that she should change her name, and be henceforth an alien from her father's family. Here she remained for more than twelve months, performing the humbler duties of the humble station to which she had been doomed, giving evidence, however, by her frequent sighs and tears, of that broken heart which the sequel of her history confirmed. One morning she had been sent out, as usual, with the box of millinery to her mistress' customers, and failing to return, after some hours of absence, she was sought for, and discovered dead in a neighbouring cottage, having purchased and taken poison to destroy herself! Her father, stricken with remorse at the consequences of his severity to his erring child, resolved to provide, in future, for the innocent offspring of her crime, and removed it from the Foundling Hospital accordingly. Of its subsequent destiny nothing is known.

took a high legal opinion, when they were advised, that owing to their departure in this respect from the spirit and letter of their charter, and the Act of Parliament confirming it, they had no chance of being protected in a court of law. *From this time, therefore, namely, January,* 1801, *no child has been received into the Hospital, either directly or indirectly, with any sum of money, large or small.*

The present practice.—The present mode of admitting children has prevailed for nearly half a century, without those variations of principle and practice which characterized previous periods of the history of the Hospital. It cannot be better set forth than in the language of a report made to Parliament ten years ago, by a commission appointed to enquire into the larger charities of London:—

"The present practice of the Governors is to decide each application for the admission of children on its own merits. There are, however, certain preliminary conditions required, the absence of any one of which is fatal to the petitioner's application, and subjects it to instant rejection, except in very peculiar cases. Thus it is required,

"1. That the child shall be illegitimate, except the father be a soldier or sailor killed in the service of his country.*

* No body of men could have been influenced by more noble and patriotic feelings, on different occasions, than the Governors of the Foundling Hospital. In 1761, during the war in Germany, also during the Continental war in 1794, and on the occasion of the battle of Waterloo, they freely opened their gates to the necessitous children of those who had fallen in the service of their country.

"2. That the child be born, and its age under twelve months.

"3. That the petitioner shall not have made an application to any parish respecting its maintenance, or have been delivered in any parish workhouse.

"4. That the petitioner shall have borne a good character previous to her misfortune or delivery.

"5. That the father shall have deserted his offspring, and be not *forthcoming*, that is, not to be found, or compellable to maintain his child.

"Supposing, therefore, that it appears by the petition, and the petitioner's examination,* that the claim for admission is advanced in respect of an illegitimate child, of a hitherto respectable parent, not twelve months old, whose father has deserted it and is not forthcoming, and whose birth has not been taken cognizance of by any parish authorities, the petitioner is considered to have established a case for inquiry; and the steward is directed to obtain information, both as to these and as to other circumstances in the case now to be stated, which differ from those above-mentioned in this respect, that none are absolutely required, and that they are all taken into consideration by the Governors, and influence their estimate of the merits of each application, according to the *degree* only in which they prevail in the individual one under consideration.

---

* "No one can blame the total change of the plan, which for the last sixty years has been made, with whatever view, by adopting the rule to admit no child whose mother does not appear to be examined."—*Lord Brougham's Letter to Sir Samuel Romilly on Charities.*

"Thus the petitioner's child acquires a stronger claim to admission, according to the degree in which it appears.

"1. That the petitioner is poor, and has no relations able or willing to maintain her child.

"2. That her delivery and shame are known to few persons, being either her relations or inmates of the house in which the circumstances occurred.

"3. That in the event of the child being received, the petitioner has a prospect of preserving her station in society, and obtaining by her own exertions an honest livelihood.

"The most meritorious case, therefore, would be one in which a young woman, having no means of subsistence, except those derived from her own labour, and having no opulent relations, previously to committing the offence bore an irreproachable character, but yielded to artful and long-continued seduction, and an express promise of marriage; whose delivery took place in secret, and whose shame was known to only one or two persons, as, for example, the medical attendant and a single relation; and, lastly, whose employers or other persons were able and desirous to take her into their service, if enabled again to earn her livelihood by the reception of her child.

"This is considered the most eligible case, and others are deemed by the Governors more or less so, in proportion as they approach nearer to or recede further from that above stated; their great object being, as they allege, to fulfil to the utmost the benevolent views of the principal Founder of the Hospital, who, as it appears by his petition for the charter, was chiefly solicitous that the mothers of illegitimate children should have other means within their reach of hiding their shame than the destruction of their miserable offspring, and thus they say they seek 'to hide the shame of the mother as well as to preserve the life of the child.'"

The first sympathies of the human heart are doubtless excited by the presence of misery, originating in what may be termed the *accidents* of life, unassisted either by the transgression or omission of the individual. Distress thus obtained, has at all times received, though not systematically, the compassionate alleviation which it requires. But there is misery of another class, which has its origin in the moral weaknesses of our nature: this, though more poignant than the former, inasmuch as it is followed by the bitterness of acknowledged transgression, did not in darker ages receive, because to human wisdom it did not seem to deserve, the commiseration of mankind. But the Christian religion, by its admirable precepts and influences, has imbued the social system of nations with a policy, which is founded on a compassionate estimate of the weaknesses of humanity, and a just measure of relief to voluntary repentance. This lesson of mercy was eminently taught by the Founder of Christianity himself, when he bade the Jew who was without sin cast the first stone at the repentant adultress, and then calmly dismissed her with the charge to *sin no more!** It was not that her crime was venial, but He who desired not the death of a sinner, but rather that she should repent and live, saw in this wretched criminal, sufficient of remorse to be the object of a lesson to mankind,—that the rigour of human law should not be exercised without a humane regard to the circumstances under which crime may have been committed, and to the sincerity of the atonement which may have followed.

It may be asked, then, where is the man, imbued with Christian charity, who is prepared to take up the stone and fling it at the poor victim of unprincipled seduction and brutal desertion? Is he ready to bear in like manner the consequences of his own guilt, and to go down the stream of life with her in her shattered bark? No:—and yet there are certain pseudo-moralists, afflicted with an unfortunate ob-

---

* Moore's poetical paraphrase of this subject naturally recurs to the mind:—

"Oh, woman! if by simple wile
Thy soul has stray'd from honour's track,
'Tis mercy only can beguile,
By gentle ways, the wand'rer back.

"The stain that on thy virtue lies,
Wash'd by thy tears, may yet decay;
As clouds that sully morning skies,
May all be wept in show'rs away.

"Go, go—be innocent, and live—
The tongues of men may wound thee sore;
But heav'n in pity can forgive,
And bids thee 'Go, and sin no more!'"

liquity of the mind's eye, who, rather than succour the necessities of one whose misfortune originated in evil, would hurl the offender headlong into perdition. Alas! the descent from virtue to vice is so easy, that but one step intervenes between them: and often, when we think we are secure, our foot slips, and we are involved in all the misery and degradation of sin! This is the fate of us all: 'tis the fate of him who proudly glories in his own rectitude: for what is the moral history of a man's life? 'Tis but a succession from virtue to vice, from vice to repentance. Shall man, then, who is so weak as not to be able to sustain his own virtue, withhold from a wretched woman, who by wily arts has been deceived, that compassion for her error which he requires for himself? And yet, those who oppose an institution founded on such principles and practice as the Foundling Hospital is now conducted, answer by their conduct the very affirmative of this question. We ask in the language of an eminent writer,* "Have faults no extenuations? Is there no difference betwixt one propensely going out of the road, and continuing there through depravity of will,—and a hapless wanderer straying by delusion, and warily treading back her steps?" The latter are the peculiar objects of the Foundling Hospital; and what Christian—what man is there who will gainsay the humanity of such an institution?

* Sterne, who preached a sermon for the charity, in the chapel of the Hospital, in 1761.

But there are certain individuals who endeavour to smother their humanity under the plea, that the policy—*the good of society* as they term it—is against the existence of any institution which shall relieve distress arising out of an evil action. Now it may be well to answer these rigid interpreters by enquiring, how far *the good of society* is injured by the institution of an asylum for the protection of infants, whose wretched parents, first straying by delusion, warily tread back their steps?

We know that *shame* is sometimes so powerful a monitor in the female breast, that it is impossible to resist its influence. Suppose then, the victim of seduction,—deceived, deserted, without even the shadow of hope in the distance to point to her relief:—suppose, we say, this wretched creature overtaken by despair, and in a fit of madness to become the murderess of her infant! we ask, how is the *good of society* answered by driving her to this desperate act? Would it not have been better secured by an opposite course? In the first place, by rescuing the infant from destruction, through the medium of some public asylum, it might be enabled hereafter to give its modicum of strength for the benefit of that public, through whose compassion it might have been saved. And secondly, by preserving the wretched parent from so desperate a crime, she might by her penitence and future rectitude have maintained the cause of virtue, and once more enjoyed the pleasure of reputation after having tasted the ill consequences of losing it.

But we will suppose that the delirium of her despair does not reach to so great a height: we will take it for granted, that nature asserts so powerfully her claims, that this victim of seduction is ready to brave all consequences for the preservation of her offspring. How can she do this?—she dare not apply to her relations:—they would reject and despise her. Her seducer has placed himself out of the reach of the law,—she has no means within herself—no hope! Being therefore unable to afford protection to her offspring in an *honest* way, she throws off for ever her remaining mantle of virtue and abandons herself to a prostituted life! Is *the good of society* promoted by her swelling the awful lists of public prostitutes? Is it promoted by her bringing up her child in the path of vice instead of virtue? No. And yet we are told by these spurious moralists, that it is unwise to step in between a hapless female and the punishment of lasting infamy which they would allot to her offence.

"Curse on the savage and unbending law
Of stern society, that turns a speck
In woman to an everlasting flaw!
And far from whisp'ring us to save or check
Her course in wantonness, bids us draw
Round her, like wretches hov'ring round a wreck,
All that the wave hath spar'd, to spoil and plunder,
And sink the noble vessel farther under."

Many are the indirect testimonies given by men of talent in favour both of the policy and humanity towards which the objects of the Foundling Hospital are directed. Fielding, who had a profound knowledge of human nature and human action, puts into the mouth of Mr. Allworthy, in his inimitable novel of "Tom Jones," the most benevolent, and at the same time the most sensible reasons for sheltering and befriending the supposed mother of the little foundling; and in his parting admonition to her, makes the good man say, "I have talked thus to you, child, not to insult you for what is past and irrecoverable, but to caution and strengthen you for the future. Nor should I have taken this trouble, but from some opinion of your good sense, notwithstanding the dreadful slip you have made, and from some hopes of your hearty repentance, which are founded on the openness and sincerity of your confession." And when her enemies would have sacrificed her to ruin and infamy, by a shameful correction in a bridewell, "so far" (says the author), "from complying with this their inclination, by which all hopes of reformation would have been abolished, and even the gate shut against her, if her own inclination should ever hereafter lead her to choose the road of virtue, Mr. Allworthy rather chose to encourage the girl to return thither by the only possible means; *for* (he adds), *too true I am afraid it is, that many women have become abandoned, and have sunk to the last degree of vice, by being unable to retrieve the first slip.*"

In the same strain the celebrated Dr. Burn* la-

* Author of "Burn's Justice."

ments the abandonment of erring females, by which (he says) "they become desperate and profligate, and are induced to make a trade of that vice, which at first was a pitiable weakness." Surely the testimony of such men in favour of the preservation of God's creatures from destruction, is of infinitely greater value than all the theories of political economists!

The late Rev. Sydney Smith, who, from the office he held, as one of the preachers in the Chapel of the Hospital, was well acquainted with the "working" of it, thus writes:—

"A very unfounded idea exists in the minds of some men little acquainted with the principles on which we proceed, that the doors of this Hospital are flung open to the promiscuous reception of infants, and that every mother can here find an asylum for her offspring, whatever be her pretensions as a virtuous mother, an indigent mother, or a mother striving by every exertion of industry to give to her children creditable support. If this were so, this institution would aim directly, and in the most unqualified manner, at the destruction of two virtues on which the happiness of society principally depends—the affection of parents, and the virtue of women. We should be counteracting, under the name of charity, all those omnipotent principles of exertion founded on the love of offspring;—we should be weakening that sacred resolution to watch, to toil, and to meet all dangers, to suffer all pains, rather than children should know the shadow of a grief, or endure but an instant of sorrow;—we should be whispering into the ear of poverty the most pernicious of all precepts;—we should be inviting them to relax from the noblest efforts, to blunt the finest feelings, and to disobey the highest commandments of Almighty God. My brethren, these things are not so: our zeal is combined with greater knowledge; and experience has taught us, that the designs of the pious demand a circumspection not inferior to that with which the machinations of the wicked are pursued. No child drinks of our cup or eats of our bread whose reception, upon the whole, we are not certain to be more conducive than pernicious to the interests of religion and good morals. We hear no mother whom it would not be merciless and shocking to turn away; we exercise the trust reposed in us with a trembling and sensitive conscience; we do not think it enough to say, This woman is wretched, and betrayed, and forsaken; but we calmly reflect if it be expedient that her tears should be dried up, her loneliness sheltered, and all her wants receive the ministration of charity. The object has uniformly been to distinguish between hardened guilt and the first taint of vice. By sheltering and protecting once, to reclaim for ever after, and not to doom to eternal infamy for one single stain of guilt.

"The fair and just way to estimate degrees of guilt is to oppose them to degrees of temptation; and no one can know more perfectly than the conductors of this charity, the abominable artifices by which the poor women who come to them for relief have been ruined, and the cruelty with which they have been abandoned. My brethren, do not believe that these are the mere casualties of vice, and the irregularities of passion, which, though well governed in the main, degenerate into occasional excess. The mothers whom we relieve have been too often ruined by systematic profligacy—by men, the only object and occupation of whose life it is to discover innocence, and to betray it. There are men in this great city who live only for such a purpose, who are the greatest and most dreadful curses that the earth carries upon its surface. My dear brethren, if I were to show you in this church the figure of a wretched woman, a brutal, shameless creature, clothed in rags, and mouldering with disease;—if I were to tell you she had once been good and happy, that she once had that chance of salvation which we all have this day;—if I were to show you the man who had doomed her to misery in this world, and to hell in the world to come, what would your feelings be? If I were to bring you another as sick and as wretched as her, and were to point out the same man as the cause of her ruin, how would your indignation rise? But if I were to tell you that the constant occupations of this man were to search for innocence and to ruin it; that he was a seducer by profession; that the only object for which he existed was to gratify his infamous passions at every expense of human happiness, would you not say that his life was too bad for the mercy of God? If the earth were to yawn for him as it yawned for Dathan and Abiram, is there one eye would be lifted up to ask for mercy for his soul? It is from such wretches as these that we strive to rescue unhappy women, to bring them back to God, to secure them from the scorn of the world that would break their hearts, and drive them into the deepest gulf of sin. But this is not all: to the cruelty of seduction is generally added the baseness of abandoning its object,—of leaving to perish in rags and in hunger a miserable woman, bribed by promises and oaths of eternal protection and regard. Now, my brethren, let us be just even to sinners; let us be merciful even to seducers in the midst of horror for their crimes; let us fix before our eyes every circumstance that can extenuate them; let us place by the side of the guilt the temptation, and judge them as we hope to be judged at a perilous season by the great Judge of us all. Let us call seduction the effect of youth and passion, still we have a right to expect all that compensation of good which youth and passion commonly afford, if we allow to them all the indulgence they usually require; but what of youth or passion is there in forgetting the unprotected weakness of women—in starving a creature whom you have ruined—in flying from her for fear she should ask you for bread? Does youth thus unite fervour with meanness? Does it, without a single compensatory virtue, combine its own vices and the vices of every other period of life? Is it violent and sordid, avaricious and impassioned, the slave of every other feeling, and the master of generous compassion alone? This is not youth; this has nothing to do with the origin of life:—it is cold and callous profligacy begun in brutal sensuality, fostered by irreligion, strengthened by association with bad men, and become so hardened, that it laughs at the very misery it creates. These are the feelings, and these the men, whose cruelty we are obliged to alleviate, and whose victims we are destined to save. Is there any friend to virtue, however rigid, who can say that such an application of charity, so scrupulous and so discriminating, is not a solid augmentation of human happiness? that it does not extend the dominion of the Gospel, and narrow the boundaries of sin? But let those who conceive that the claims even of such unhappy women should be rejected, consider what it is they do reject: they reject the weakness of sex; they are deaf to the voice of ruined innocence; they refuse assistance to youth, shuddering at the gulf of infamy; they would turn out an indigent mother to the merciless world, at a period when she demands all that charity can afford, or compassion feel! But whatever be the crimes of the parents, and whatever views different individuals may take of the relief extended to them, there is no man who thinks that the children should perish for their crimes, or that those shall be doomed to suffer any misery who can have committed no fault. Therefore this part of the institution is as free from the shadow of blame as every other part is free from the reality."

Sir Thomas Bernard, Baronet, who was for some years Treasurer of the Hospital, writes as follows in 1803*:—

"The preserving and educating so many children, which without the Foundling Hospital would have been lost to that society of which they are calculated to become useful members, is certainly a great and public benefit. The adoption of a helpless unprotected infant, the watching over its progress to maturity, and fitting it to be useful to itself and others here, and to attain eternal happiness hereafter, these are no common or ordinary acts of beneficence; but their value and their importance are lost, when compared with the benefits which (without any prejudice to the original objects of the Charity), the mothers derive from this Institution, as it is at present conducted. The preserving the mere vital functions of an infant cannot be put in competition with saving from vice, misery, and infamy, a young woman, in the bloom of life, whose crime may have been a single and solitary act of indiscretion. Many extraordinary cases of repentance, followed by restoration to peace, comfort, and reputation, have come within the knowledge of the writer of this note. Some cases have occured, within his own observation, of wives happily placed, the mothers of thriving families, who, but for the saving aid of this Institution, might have become the most noxious and abandoned prostitutes. Very rare are the instances,

---

Vide Report of the Society for Bettering the Condition of the Poor.

none has come within notice, of a woman relieved by the Foundling Hospital, and not thereby preserved from a course of prostitution."*

There are 500 children supported by the Hospital, from extreme infancy up to the age of fifteen. This is the maximum number for the maintenance of which the present funds can be made available. It is only therefore as vacancies occur by apprenticeship or death, reducing this number, that other children can be received. The average admissions per annum for the last five years was forty-four. The average number of applications for the admission of children was 181. Independently, therefore, of a principle of action which governs the Committee in the selection of cases, the limited means at their disposal, as compared with the claims upon them, furnishes of itself a safe-guard or guarantee against a too free administration of this, the most important branch of the establishment.

---

* The Compiler of this Book, from his peculiar position in the Hospital as the investigator of petitions for the admission of children, has had, perhaps, for some years past, better opportunities than any one else of observing the operations of the charity as affecting the unfortunate mothers of the children, and he can confidently assert (with Sir Thomas Bernard), that however obvious and unquestionable may be the advantages of such an institution in nurturing and educating a large number of innocent, and, otherwise, destitute children, this is only *secondary* to the decided and certain benefits derived by their deluded and repentant mothers, and, through them, by the society of which they are members. He has witnessed, with an interest which has made an indelible impression upon his mind, numbers of instances where the peace and happiness of a whole family have been restored by relieving one erring member of the object of her and their disgrace!

It has been said (and gravely, though ridiculously, charged against the Hospital) that the Governors are liable to be deceived, and that in some cases they have been imposed upon by designing persons. This may be so, it being the fate of all *human* institutions to be imperfect. Judges and juries are very often betrayed into error by false witnesses, but does any one pretend to assert that therefore, courts of justice are useless? If the duration of institutions, of whatever nature, was to depend upon the perfect integrity of their administration, it is to be feared that their existence would be short-lived indeed!

THE PRIVILEGES OF THE GOVERNORS.

There is a class of men with so little charity in their hearts, as to make it an incomprehensible matter to them how any individual can be found, in this mercenary world, to contribute either his time or money to benevolent purposes without some commensurate benefit to himself; but it is a fact, notwithstanding, that there is a large body of individuals (and miserable indeed would society be without such persons), who from the purest motives of Christian charity, are to be found dispensing the good with which God has blest them, for the benefit of their poorer sojourners in this world of sin and misery, divested entirely of self-interest. Of that number are the Governors of the Foundling Hospital! It is asserted without fear of contradiction, by one who has had for many years ample opportunity of ascertaining it, that there is not a charity in or out of the metropolis, more *disinterestedly* administered in the selection of its objects than this institution. It has become a *principle* (fully supported in *practice*), that no Governor shall interfere, either directly or indirectly, by recommendation or otherwise, in obtaining the admission of a child. No interest is exercised except what the abstract misery of the case on its presentation excites, and all extraneous support is set aside. The truth is (and this is a good feature of the charity), that the persons relieved are of that class who are unable to command patronage, or who dare not seek it lest their error and their misery should be betrayed!

This disinterested administration of the most important branch of such an institution is thus asserted, because there is a "vulgar error" on the subject, namely—that the Governors have the privilege of *presenting* children, after the manner of other establishments; but a more unfounded statement never was erroneously conceived or ignorantly disseminated!

NAMING AND BAPTIZING OF THE CHILDREN.

It has been the practice of the Governors, from the earliest period of the Hospital to the present time, to name the children at their own will and pleasure, whether their parents should have been known or not.

At the baptism of the children first taken into the Hospital, which was on the 29th March, 1741, it is recorded, that "there was at the ceremony a fine appearance of persons of quality and distinction: his Grace the Duke of Bedford, our President, their Graces the Duke and Duchess of Richmond, the Countess of Pembroke, and several others, honouring the children with their names, and being their sponsors."

Thus the register of this period presents the courtly names of Abercorn, Bedford, Bentinck, Montague, Marlborough, Newcastle, Norfolk, Pomfret, Pembroke, Richmond, Vernon, &c. &c., as well as those of numerous other living individuals, great and small, who at that time took an interest in the establishment. When these names were exhausted, the authorities stole those of eminent deceased personages, their first attack being upon the church. Hence we have a Wickliffe, Huss, Ridley, Latimer, Laud, Sancroft, Tillotson, Tennison, Sherlock, &c. &c. Then come the mighty dead of the poetical race, viz.—Geoffrey Chaucer, William Shakspeare, John Milton, &c. Of the philosophers, Francis Bacon stands pre-eminently conspicuous. As they proceeded, the Governors were more warlike in their notions, and brought from their graves Philip Sidney, Francis Drake, Oliver Cromwell, John Hampden, Admiral Benbow, and Cloudesley Shovel. A more peaceful list followed this, viz.—Peter Paul Rubens, Anthony Vandyke, Michael Angelo, and Godfrey Kneller; William Hogarth, and Jane, his wife, of course not being forgotten. Another class of names was borrowed from popular novels of the day, which accounts for Charles Allworthy, Tom Jones, Sophia Western, and Clarissa Harlowe. The gentle Isaac Walton stands alone.

So long as the admission of children was confined within reasonable bounds, it was an easy matter to find names for them ; but during the "parliamentary era" of the Hospital, when its gates were thrown open to all comers, and each day brought its regiment of *infantry* to the establishment, the Governors were sometimes in difficulties ; and when this was the case, they took a zoological view of the subject, and named them after the creeping things and beasts of the earth, or created a nomenclature from various handicrafts or trades.

In 1801, the hero of the Nile and some of his friends honoured the establishment with a visit, and stood sponsors to several of the children. The names given on this occasion were Baltic Nelson, William and Emma Hamilton, Hyde Parker, &c.

Up to a very late period the Governors were sometimes in the habit of naming the children after themselves or their friends; but it was found to be an inconvenient and objectionable course, inasmuch as when they grew to man and womanhood, they were apt to lay claim to some affinity of blood with their nomenclators. The present practice therefore is, for the Treasurer to prepare a list of ordinary names, by which the children are baptized.

THE NURSING OF THE CHILDREN.

The early practice in the nursing of the children, and its results, cannot be better stated than in the language of Sir Hans Sloane, Bart., in the following letter, dated 28th October, 1748:—

"*To my very worthy and respected friend, John Milner, Esq., Vice-President of the Hospital for the Maintenance and Education of Exposed and Deserted young Children.*

"Sir,

"It is some years since I had some discourse with you upon the erection of the Hospital for the Maintenance and Education of Exposed and Deserted young Children: a thing, which being much wanted in this city, I had frequently recommended to my acquaintance, and particularly to you, who have so great a hand in taking care of all people in want, and promoting so good and necessary a work of taking care of infants, which by the management of parish nurses, in giving them diacodium, or other opiats, to quiet them when fretting with diseases occasioned by their bad nourishment, generally sweet'ned with sugar, and the want of the breast by wett nurses, scarse ever live to two years old, which is the cause of the great numbers of children of that age, who are about a third part of all those who dye yearly, of all diseases and accidents, within the bills of mortality, as may be seen by the same at St. Giles's parish, there being no wett nurses provided, but being bred up by hand, that out of foundling or other children sent thither, scarse one in seven lived, as you may very well remember. At the Temple and at Chelsea, I am assured there dyes above one half of the foundling children. What great detriment accrues from thence to the publick is easy to be understood by such who know the strength and wellfare of any nation depends on the number and health of its inhabitants. Upon this occasion you may very well call to mind, that when I was present at the first meetings of the Foundling Hospital, I was very much against, and opposed the intended method of breeding up infants by hand, but, on the contrary, urged having wett nurses for the children to be taken in there. My opinion I told you, and the rest of the Governors, was founded on the experience that I had for fifty years, that as far as my memory served me, I observed that in three infants bred without breasts, two generally dyed, or in that proportion, notwithstanding what I or others could do to help them. This, I generally thought, proceeded from deviating from the orders of God and nature, to follow men's inventions. I have allways immediately advised, in such cases, the breast, as the first and best remedy, which seldom fails, unless the child would not suck, in which case, breast-milk given with a spoon is the best remedy, by which, in some urgent cases, where children had their tongue, lips, or noses obstructed, either by diseases or accidents, before, or in the birth, their lives have been saved by receiving the same proper nourishment, though not by sucking. What deceives unthinking people is, the children taking down such artificiall succedaneous nourishment or victuals with seeming complacency: they do not consider that any infant will swallow even any poyson, that hath no ill tast, that is putt into its mouth. Mankind would be in a very bad and worse condition than other animals, if it were not to be expected that the parents should take reasonable care of them till experience, and the use of their own reason, hath taught them what is proper for them. We see, every day, most surprising instances of the care of animals in preserving, defending, providing proper nourishment, and training up their young, while they are not in a condition to act for themselves, whether from instinct or an inferior use of reason.

"The bad qualities of many wett nurses, and their opinion of being so necessary to families, hath sometimes made their masters weary of such servants, and obliged them to try what they did not so well consider or know. They did not know that the gutts of children are, some of them, not much thicker than writing paper; that the blood-vessels were, many of them, capillary, nay, even much smaller than a hair; and that a disproportion'd nourishment might occasion great disorders, not only in the *primæ viæ*, but also in the turnings, and many circumvolutions in the gutts and several glands of the body, which might occasion rickets and the king's evil, and these sort of diseases, more taken notice of in England than other countries. The infant's incapacity of judging, must by the order of nature and Providence, devolve to the parents, and seems to be pointed out for sucking, till they have teeth to tear or grind. I have seen and very much condemn'd the custom of some who, too soon, put into the hands of infants dry crusts of bread, chickens' leggs, and other obstructing nourishment; and I have seen the liveliest and healthiest children, who never had other nourishment than from the breast for upwards of one, if not two years. This too thick nourishment, in elder people, is helpd by drinking, when prompt to it by thirst, or oppression at their stomach, which children are not able to discover.

"The natural and customary time of the appearance of teeth is about eight months, if pregnancy happens, then a dry very carefull nurse may suffice, and the child wean'd ; if before, a wett nurse must be procured. I think the difference of the age of a wett nurse's milk is not to be so much regarded, having in my own family had one wett nurse suckle four children successively, who have been and now are healthy and well.

"The mischiefs that arise from want of breast-milk are gripes, from the disproportion'd food turning generally soure, giving green stools, causing pain, and irritating the gutts to discharge them, and the *mucus intestinalis* given by nature to defend them, bringing blood from the capillary vessells dispersed through some parts of it, hindering rest, and leaving them little else but skin and bone, and causing obstructions in the glands of the ventricles of the brain, and brain itself, in which I have seen an inundation from this cause, whence follows a discharge of *serum* occasioning convulsions of all sorts. I have been the more certain of this, because, considering the natural and reasonable desire in mankind to perpetuate their kind, it was necessary to see the causes of the deaths of their children; and I think I never miss'd, in many hundreds open'd, the finding it proceed from the above-mention'd causes, which blisters, bleeding, gentle purgers, aperients, and proper remedies, proved ineffectual to cure. The use that I made of this, was the preventing the like in subsequent children, by making (especially such as appeared to have any disorder) an issue at, as near as could be to, the setting on of the first *vertebre* of the neck to the skull, which I am as certain as I can be hath preserved many families from dying without heires of their bodies to inherit, some of them, very great honours and large estates.

"When loosenesses and green stools happen to infants, testaceous powders, as chalk, crabs eyes, claws, &c., helps more than rhubarb, which purges them more, and is no ways to be depended on for strengthening the bowells, as may be seen, if I remember right, by the experiments of the Academie of Sciences, in some of their memoirs, and by the daily experience of too many purging to death by it; whereas the testaceous powders, and a moderate use of diascordium, made as prescribed by Fracastorius, its original author, after each loose stool: about ten grains at a time, when necessary, is one of the best remedies, given in a spoonfull of breast-milk, or hartshorn drink.

"Another thing I have taken notice of as a great fault in the management of infants, is the putting them too soon upon their leggs, and bribing them to walk alone, or even with the help of leading-strings, which brings many crooked bones, from their not having acquired a suitable hardness to sustain, but grow crooked under the weight of their bodies, nature rather seeming to design their grovelling on their hands and feet at first, than standing erect. Most other nations have their limbs streight for that reason; and I do not remember to have seen, in whole countrys, for some years, so many crooked bones as are to be seen in half an houres passing the streets in London, not counting such as are bed-rid, confined at home, or women whose habits hide their deformities of that kind.

"If you remember, at that time, it pleased God, I fell very ill, and was not able to attend you at the meeting of the Guardians of the Foundling Hospital, who were advised to bring up by hand all such infants as would feed, and suckle only such as would not. This being much against my opinion, from the ill effects I had observed by it (as I had before told you and the rest of the Governors), made me some time after, upon my recovery, inquisitive about the event of it; when, upon examining the books of the Hospital, I found as follows, by which it plainly appears, that what I said was agreable to matter of fact:—

"March 25th, 1741—admitted 30 children; to

wett nurses, 2; dyed, ——: to dry-nurses, 28; dyed, 15.

"April 17th, 1741—admitted 30 children; to wett nurses, 7; dyed, 1: to dry nurses, 22; dyed, 11.

"May 8th, 1741—admitted 30 children; to wett nurses, 17; dyed, 4: to dry nurses, 13; dyed, 8.

"Total children admitted, 90. Total to wett nurses, 26; dyed, 5. Total to dry nurses, 63; dyed, 34. Taken out, 1.

"I am, Sir,
"Your most obedient and
"Most humble servant,
"HANS SLOANE."*

"Chelsea."

There can be no doubt that as the object of an institution of this nature is to save life, its managers should take all reasonable means for effecting such a desideratum. It is with this intention that the present Governors invariably obtain for the infants falling under their charitable care, *wet nurses,* unless it happens (which is rarely the case) that the age of a child renders such assistance unnecessary. The result, therefore, of this course is much more favour-

* Sir Hans Sloane, Bart., was of Scotch extraction, and was born at Killileagh, in the County of Down. He was an eminent physician and naturalist, and founded the British Museum. He was the author of several excellent works. Having purchased the Manor of Chelsea, he gave the Company of Apothecaries the entire freehold of their botanical garden there. Sir Hans Sloane was physician to Christ's Hospital, and on the death of Sir Isaac Newton, in 1727, he was elected president of the Royal Society. He died on the 11th January, 1752, and was buried at Chelsea.

able than that adopted at the outset of the establishment.

In considering the question of mortality, the children of the Hospital should be classed under two heads, namely :—1st, those under the age of five years in the *country*, and 2ndly, those of from five to fifteen in *London*.

With respect to the former, the chances against rearing many of them are very great, and for these reasons. The mothers of the infants (who for the most part are very young), being desirous of "hiding their shame" from their relatives, or those with whom they may happen to be placed, manage by contrivances and artifices to prevent a knowledge of their imprudence until it can no longer be concealed. The writer has known many instances where girls (for their youth justifies the designation) have been living with their mothers, with whom they have been in constant intercourse and even sleeping in the same bed, and yet have contrived to hide from their parent the fact of their unfortunate condition till the moment of confinement. In the same manner servants manage to undergo the labours of their office, and contrive to elude the observation of their mistresses, till the instant of giving birth to a child. The unnatural distortions of body by which their secret is preserved, are accompanied by anxieties of mind which does not arise only from the dread of discovery. The prospect before her is dreary enough, but the retrospect is perhaps worse. "She finds herself" (says the late Rev. John Hewlett), "the victim of treachery and voluptuousness, where she fondly hoped to be the object of pure and individual love, and at a time when the languor of the body and the growing anxiety of the mind powerfully claim, and in general receive, additional tenderness, she is obliged to endure the severest affliction that fear could imagine, or unkindness produce." Can it be wondered at therefore, that an infant born under such circumstances, should be deficient in those physical developments which otherwise it might have possessed. But this is not all. The same powerful motive which prompted her first desire to conceal her disgrace, leads her to seek the only other opportunity she has of ensuring such concealment, namely—by putting her infant away from her, as soon after its birth as possible, to some nurse, who under a promise of payment, which the mother is unable to fulfil, engages to take upon herself the duties of the parent, duties which in nine cases out of ten she neglects to perform in a satisfactory manner. Beginning life with such opposing contingencies, and thus neglected, the infant is admitted into the Foundling Hospital. "At least one-fifth of those admitted, during the last nine years" (says the examining medical officer) "have been in such a miserable state of emaciation, as to make it doubtful if they could be reared at all, and of those presented in tolerable health, many receive a serious check from the change of nurse, condition, and other circumstances attending their admission. These infants are presented at all ages, from one to twelve months, and have been mostly exposed to all the injurious consequences arising from insufficient nursing and improper diet; the greater number have not had the breast at all, and I have generally found on enquiry, that those who have had the advantage of a wet nurse, have been fed at the same time with spoon food."

The Compiler has searched the registers of the Hospital, and has extracted an account of the mortality of 100 children, during the first five years of their lives, received at two separate periods, viz.—from May, 1835, to May, 1837; and from May, 1837, to March, 1839; and he finds the following to be the result:—

				1st Period.	2nd Period.
Deaths in the	1st	year of their age	. .	12	9
,,	2nd	,,	. .	5	10
,,	3rd	,,	. .	2	2
,,	4th	,,	. .	0	0
,,	5th	,,	. .	1	0
				20	21*

The causes of death were as follows, viz.:—

Convulsions, 9; inflammation of lungs, 3; malformation of chest, 3; diarrhœa, 3; inflammation of bowels, 4; water on brain, 4; croup, 2; hydrocele, 1; disease of mesenteric glands, 5; scarlet fever, 2;

* The mortality of children in private families under five years of age in the metropolis, is between thirty and forty per cent. In agricultural districts the mortality amongst cottagers is about twenty-eight per cent.

atrophy, 1; bilious vomiting, 1; scrofula, 1; hooping cough, 1; teething, and the breaking of a blood-vessel, 1.

The above, therefore, furnishes evidence of the loss of life, per centum, of those children under the age of five years, whilst at nurse in the *country*.

The following is the account of the mortality of the children of the Hospital, in *London*, during a period of ten years, from the ages of five to fifteen:—

	Average number of Children in the House.	Deaths.
1837	216	3
1838	216	0
1839	230	0
1840	226	0
1841	237	1
1842	223	12*
1843	258	2
1844	298	0
1845	305	2
1846	307	1

The diseases of which the said children died are as follows:—

Water on the head, 2; consumption, 1; scrofula,

* This extraordinary mortality caused much anxiety to the eminent medical staff of the establishment, and it was attended with unusual circumstances. The epidemic with which the children were attacked was that of measles and hooping cough, co-existing in many cases, and complicated with severe and extensive inflammation of the lungs, coupled from the commencement, with a degree of prostration of strength which made the indications of treatment peculiarly perplexing and contradictory. The number of children afflicted with the epidemic was nearly 100.

1; disease of mesenteric glands, 1; bronchitis, terminating in low fever, 1; disease of the spine, and gangrene of the lungs, 1; chronic peritonitis, 1; typhus fever, 1; scarlet fever, 1; dropsy, following scarlet fever, 1; measles and hooping cough complicated with inflammation of lungs or bowels, 10.

The general health of the children within the walls of the Hospital is remarkably good; and with the exception of occasional epidemic visitations, they have been singularly free from the acute forms of disease to which children in general are so liable.

Perhaps the healthiness of the locality could not be better exemplified than by this fact—that several adult foundlings, who from some organic defect, have from time to time become chargeable to the Hospital for life, and have scarcely ever quitted the walls of the building, have lived to a very advanced period--some dying between the ages of seventy and eighty years, and others between eighty and ninety.

THE DISPOSAL OF THE CHILDREN.

The children are all disposed of by *apprenticeship*. the girls at the age of fifteen to domestic service, for a term of five years, and the boys at the age of fourteen as mechanics, &c. for a term of seven years. The trades to which the latter have been apprenticed during the *last* seven years are as follows, viz.:— tailors, sixteen; boot and shoe makers, sixteen; fishermen, seven; cabinet makers, four; linen drapers, three; confectioners, two; bakers, two; gold beaters, two; hair dressers, three; hair manufacturers, two; silver smith, one; opticians, two; tin plate worker and ironmonger, one; general provision dealer, one; weaver, one; law writers, two; watch maker, one; pawnbrokers, three; soda water manufacturer, one; cooper, one; dyer, one; paper hanger, one; furnishing undertaker, one; brass, copper, and iron wire drawer, one; silk hat manufacturer, one; domestic service, four; in all eighty apprentices. A very satisfactory report was recently made of their conduct and destination, *four* only excepted. These have left their masters, owing to disagreements, but are believed to be leading reputable lives.

With respect to the girls, it appeared by a recent investigation, that of all those apprenticed during the last five years, there was only *one* whose conduct had been faulty, and she was redeeming her character by subsequent good behaviour.

THE REVENUE OF THE HOSPITAL.

There is much misconception and misunderstanding on the part of the public on this head.

In the memoir of Captain Coram, it has been clearly shewn that what property he had acquired, was consumed in the pursuit of his philanthropic projects, and that he had no wealth by which to endow, even in a limited degree, an institution of this nature, being himself a recipient of charity for the last two years of his life. The Hospital had nothing therefore to depend upon at its commencement, but the eleemosynary aid of the public, either in the form of donations or legacies; and what permanent revenue it now has, may be ascribed to the fortuitous policy of the early Governors and the provident care of their successors. Thus the Governors in 1741, being in pursuit of a salubrious site for erecting an Hospital, fixed upon certain fields in the neighbourhood of London, deriving their name from "Lamb's Conduit,"* (in extent fifty-six acres) belonging to the Earl of Salisbury, who agreed to sell

* "William Lamb, some time a gentleman of the Chapel to Henry VIII, citizen and clothworker, having drawn together several springs of water into a head, now from him denominated Lamb's Conduit, near the Foundling Hospital, at the upper end of Red Lion Street, in High Holborn; whence in a leaden pipe two thousand yards long, he conveyed the same to Snow Hill; where having re-edified a ruinous conduit long disused (and now entirely demolished), he laid his water into the same, to the great advantage and convenience of that neighbourhood. This conduit finished March 26th, 1577, though removed a little from its place, still retains the name of its re-builder, the charge whereof, together with that of the other parts of the work, amounted to £1500."—*Maitland's London.*

Great Ormond Street, leading out of "Lamb's Conduit" Street, was formerly the place of residence of several eminent judges and literary men, and the "Foundling Estate," till towns were built beyond it, was the favourite suburban retreat of merchants and lawyers. As the district is getting old enough to deserve a chronicler, the origin of the names of the squares and streets may be recorded. Brunswick and Mecklenburgh Squares had their existence in an effusion of loyalty on the part of the Governors of the Hospital. Guildford Street was named after a noble president of the Charity. Great Coram Street after the founder. Hunter Street after John Hunter, Esq. Wilmot Street ftom John Wilmot, Esq. Everett Street from Thomas Everett, Esq., M.P. Heathcote Street from Michael Heathcote, Esq. (Vice-Presidents). Bernard Street from Sir Thomas Bernard, Bart., and Compton Street from Samuel Compton Cox, Esq. (Treasurers). Kenton Street from B Kenton, Esq. (a Governor). The rest of the Streets were named after leading public individuals, &c.

them to the charity for £5500. The whole tract of land was purchased out of casual benefactions and legacies, not because the charity required it for its then purposes, but because the Earl would not sell any fractional part of it. As London increased, it approached this property, and the Governors were induced fifty-five years after, to turn that to the pecuniary advantage of the charity, which its early managers had not the remotest idea would have ever become otherwise beneficial than as guaranteeing the healthy condition of the children. From this accidental circumstance, the Governors derive from ground rents alone, an annual income equal to the purchase-money! This income is secured by leases of ninety-nine years duration, of which there is an average unexpired term of forty-five years, so that until that period, the income from this source must remain the same.

Some imaginative persons have invested the Hospital already with the property in which it has only a remote reversionary interest, and they unwisely withhold their charitable hands, not because they disapprove of the Institution, but because it is already so rich! No charity can be rich unless it has a surplus revenue after every reasonable opportunity has offered for disposing of it upon the objects for whose benefit it was created. This is not the case with the Foundling Hospital. "It confines itself," (says Bishop Thirlwall), "to a particular class of cases, one, however, which is unhappily so large, that it constantly overgrows the means of relief." It should be understood, therefore, that to these ground-rents, and the interest of certain stock, which has been nursed by the great care of the Guardians of the Charity, to the benefactions at the chapel doors and other such casualties, the Hospital is wholly dependent for support, and will be so for nearly fifty years to come.

The walls of the building present, it is true, a goodly array of tablets, noting very considerable benefactions and legacies, but it should be recollected that the greater part of this money was swallowed up in the vortex caused by Parliamentary interference, and that only during the last fifty years have the Governors been able to lay up for the Hospital a pecuniary foundation.

The present annual income may be stated as follows:—

Rents of the Estates	£5520
Interest on £108,388, Stock . . .	3307
Benefactions on an average of 3 years .	241
Net Produce of the Chapel on an average of 3 years	687
	£9755

Of those who were early benefactors, the name of Omychund, a black merchant of Calcutta, should be specially mentioned. He bequeathed to the Foundling and Magdalen Hospitals, 37,500 current rupees, to be equally divided; but unfortunately a portion only of this munificent legacy could be extracted from the grasp of Huzzorimal, his executor, notwithstanding the zealous interference of Warren Hastings, Esq., the Governor-General, and other eminent functionaries.

The following is a legacy of another kind. The testator was one Shirley, of Stratford in Essex.

"The whole of my Dramatic Works, consisting of nine Tragedies, one Comedy, and five smaller productions, I bequeath to the Governors of the Foundling Hospital, in trust for that greatly useful Institution, hoping their being enabled to get them performed, unaltered or mutilated, in one of the London Theatres, they being certainly not inferior to any set of such performances produced at the present age; and should they be acted, I request the repayment out of the profits to all subscribers to me, which can amount but to a small sum of money."

In 1759, William Williams, Esq., who possessed property in Jamaica, bequeathed the same to certain persons "*in trust to sell the same, together with all and every the Negro, Mulatto, and other slaves whatsoever to me belonging, with their future offspring, issue, or increase, and to pay the net proceeds to the Treasurer of the Foundling Hospital.*" His next bequest is as follows:—"*Item, I give and bequeath to that most abandonedly wicked, vile, detestable rogue and impostor, who hath assumed, and now does, or lately did go by the name of Gersham Williams, pretending to be a son of mine, one shilling only, to buy him an halter, where-*

with to hang himself, being what he hath for a long, long, very long while past meritted and deserved from the law of the hands of the hangman, for his great and manifold villanies."

At the demise of his reputed father, this "Gersham Williams," made many attempts to compromise matters with the Governors of the Hospital regarding the legacy, but he proved a slippery character, and failed in his object. The legacy yielded to the Charity £5563.

THE BENEVOLENT FUND.

As this Memoranda was *commenced* with a view to its publication being made the medium for increasing the usefulness of the above Fund, it seems desirable that it should *conclude* with some notice of the object of its establishment.

The Fund was set on foot in the year 1845, by several of the acting Governors of the Hospital on this humane principle, viz:—That the helplessness of old age, especially when accompanied by an irreproachable life, was as worthy an object of compassion and amelioration as the helplessness of infancy, and that sickness, unprovoked by intemperance or other misconduct, deserved in the after life of the objects of the charity, as much alleviation as it received in the days of their youth. In fact, that as the Institution rescued them in childhood from want, or from the cold and compulsory charity of a parish workhouse, so in old age or sickness should it extend its merciful hand for the same object.

The Fund is dispensed by granting weekly allowances to the aged and infirm, and by affording temporary relief to the distressed.

It is wholly supported by subscription, the revenues of the Hospital not being applicable for the purpose.

It contributes to the maintenance of ten weekly pensioners, but, although there are other claimants, its limited means will not admit at present of an extension of its operations. The aggregate ages of four of these recipients amount to 339 years.

Of one of them, aged 90 (who in manner and conduct may be taken as a specimen of the whole), the compiler is enabled to give the following interesting account in the language of an active Governor of the Hospital and a zealous and liberal friend of the Fund.

"St. John Street,
"10th November, 1846.

"My dear Mr. Brownlow,

"During my brief stay at Warrington, I thought it a duty incumbent on me to seek out our venerable pensioner on the Benevolent Fund, Bernard Harris, for which purpose I introduced myself to the lady who takes so warm an interest in his welfare, and who, upon my expressing a desire to see him, very kindly accompanied me to his cottage. I found the poor old man in bed, to which he had been confined for the last six weeks; upon his being informed who

I was, and the object of my visit, his feelings were much overcome; he held my hand tightly within his own, and it was some minutes ere he could speak to me; he then with much emotion, said, 'I thank God for giving me this opportunity of expressing my unbounded gratitude for all the care and attention bestowed on me in infancy: but for the protection of the Foundling Hospital, I might have been brought up in a career of misery and vice, and become an outcast. The Hospital sheltered me in childhood, gave me instruction—apprenticed me to a weaver, by means of which I have not only obtained an honest livelihood, but have brought up and maintained a family; and now, when with the exception of one daughter, all my children are dispersed, and I have reached my ninetieth year, and am about to descend into the grave, I find my last days rendered comfortable by means of the Foundling Benevolent Fund, and which has thus in my old age saved me from the horrors and degradation of the Union Poor House. I am of a great age, but I am not afraid to die, no, I am patiently waiting God's good pleasure, and my last words shall be a prayer to Him, to bless that noble institution where I was taught to love and fear him.'

"I asked him to inform me something of his history, which he cheerfully complied with; and upon enquiring if he had ever visited the Hospital since he left it, he replied that not only had he done so, but it was ever nearest his thoughts, as a proof of which he told me that some years since he addressed a letter to the Governors of the Hospital, and was so gratified by the feeling manifested towards him in the reply, that he had learned it by rote, and would repeat it to me, which he did without the slightest hesitation. He however gave me a much more gratifying proof of his retentive memory, by repeating without any mistake or misplacement of words, the Instructions given to Foundling apprentices upon leaving the Hospital; upon coming to that part which says, 'be not ashamed that you were bred in this Hospital. Own it: and say that it was through the good Providence of Almighty God, that you were taken care of. Bless Him for it,' the old man lifted himself in bed, and with much energy, said, 'I am *not* ashamed of it,—I *do* bless Him for it.'

"I then enquired into his circumstances, and found that in consequence of his now being confined to his bed, his daughter was obliged to give up her attendance at a neighbouring factory, where she had been enabled to earn a few shillings a week, in order to devote herself entirely to the care of her father, and thus their means had become more straitened since his illness. I told him that the character which I had received of himself and daughter was so satisfactory in every respect, that notwithstanding the Benevolent Fund was so limited as to prevent our carrying out its objects to the extent required, yet I would intercede with the Committee to increase his small allowance, by an additional grant of two shillings a week, for which I assure you he seemed most grateful. I must add that his cottage, although very humble, was remarkably neat and clean.

"I took my leave deeply impressed with what I had witnessed, and felt how much *you*, who had laboured so assiduously in establishing this Fund, might congratulate yourself upon its happy results, administering as it does to the aged and necessitous Foundlings in the last days of their existence.

"Believe me,

"Yours very faithfully,

"W. FOSTER WHITE."

In concluding this Memoranda, the Compiler begs to state that these records have caused him some *trouble*, but that he shall consider it no trouble at all to receive the contributions of the reader in aid of the Benevolent Fund of the Foundling Hospital.

[F. WARR, Printer, Red Lion Passage.]

For EU product safety concerns, contact us at Calle de José Abascal, 56–1°, 28003 Madrid, Spain or eugpsr@cambridge.org.

www.ingramcontent.com/pod-product-compliance
Ingram Content Group UK Ltd.
Pitfield, Milton Keynes, MK11 3LW, UK
UKHW010039140625
459647UK00012BA/1484

* 9 7 8 1 1 0 8 0 5 4 8 3 6 *